DESTROYER
CAPTAIN

DESTROYER CAPTAIN

LESSONS OF A
FIRST COMMAND

Adm. James G. Stavridis

Naval Institute Press
Annapolis, Maryland

Naval Institute Press
291 Wood Road
Annapolis, MD 21402

Library of Congress Cataloging-in-Publication Data

Stavridis, James.
  Destroyer captain : lessons of a first command / Adm.
James Stavridis.
      p. cm.
  ISBN 978-1-59114-849-4 (alk. paper)
  1. Stavridis, James. 2. United States. Navy--Biography. 3.
Admirals--United States--Biography. I. Title.
V63.S73A1 2008
359.0092--dc22
[B]

                                        2007032046

Printed in the United States of America on acid-free paper

14 13 12 11 10 09 08   9 8 7 6 5 4 3 2
First Printing

FOR LAURA

CONTENTS

Preface   ix

Destroyer Captain   1

Epilogue   195

About the Author   201

Photos follow page 116

PREFACE

————

When I was assigned to my first command at sea in
1993, I decided to keep a journal. I never thought
it would be something I would publish. Rather, I
intended it to be a sort of personal memoir of what I hoped
would be an interesting and productive time in my life.

I was in my mid-thirties when I was initially detailed to the
USS *Barry*, a brand-new *Arleigh Burke*–class Aegis guided-
missile destroyer. I was married to Laura, a wonderful and
Navy-experienced wife, and we had two small daughters—
both under the age of ten. I knew that the hardest part of the
job by far would be the immense amount of time I would
spend away from the three of them, sailing from the ship's
home port of Norfolk, Virginia. Yet, it was very clear to me
that this command was something I wanted to do and had
been preparing to undertake for over twenty years, since I
walked through the gates at Annapolis and entered the U.S.
Naval Academy in the hot, humid summer of 1972.

The *Barry* was recently commissioned, and I would be
only the second commanding officer, an enviable position
indeed. Serving as the second skipper of a warship is usually
thought to be the best spot for the simple reason that the first
CO is charged with "building the ship" through the long construction process, while the second captain generally has the
far more enjoyable task of taking the ship forward on her first

deployment. Such was the case for me in the *Barry*, and I was truly excited.

Arleigh Burke–class destroyers are built from the keel up to fight. They are largely constructed of solid steel after some unhappy experimentation by the Navy with more aluminum in the hull and masts in early ships during the late twentieth century. The ships are outfitted with the formidable Aegis combat system. Aegis, which means "shield" in Greek, is a complex suite of sensors, weapons, and command/control elements that collectively permit the ship to track targets in the air, on the sea, and under the water for many miles around the vessel. Notably, the air search radar systems can find incoming missiles and aircraft at distances up to 250 miles (and beyond, when used against ballistic missiles). The ship also carries a large number of long-range missiles, including the deadly Standard air defense missile and the long-range land-attack Tomahawk missile.

The crew numbers about 340. The *Barry* shifted from having only men in the crew to a mixed group, with approximately 15 percent women, about halfway through my tour. She was the first destroyer in the Navy to embark women as part of the crew, and their successful integration was a significant achievement for the ship. Without question, the very best and most enjoyable part of commanding a U.S. Navy warship in the all-volunteer force is interacting with the young men and women who crew her. They are in every sense of the word inspirational, and a major part of this memoir is their story as well. The namesake for the class, Adm. Arleigh Burke, a fighting admiral of the Second World War, often said that "our young Sailors, commissioned officers and enlisted, are the best of us all, and the hope of our future as well." I could not agree more after a lifetime of service with so many of them at sea.

The mid-1990s were a trying time for the U.S. Navy. We were dramatically reducing the number of ships in the fleet as part of the post–Cold War drawdown, and as a result, the remaining ships—especially the surface ships like mine—were sailing with great frequency. As you will discover in the course of this story, I would eventually sail well over 150,000 nautical miles at sea. The *Barry* would play a role in world events, including the UN operations off Haiti in the fall of 1993, the embargo operations off the Balkans in the summer of 1994, and the response to Saddam Hussein's ill-fated thrust toward Kuwait in the fall of that same year.

The ship would also sail on countless training and exercise evolutions, make many port visits in the interest of diplomacy, and show the U.S. flag throughout the Caribbean Sea, Atlantic Ocean, Mediterranean and Red seas, and the Arabian Gulf. We were out of our home port—and away from our families—nearly 75 percent of the time during the twenty-seven months I was in command. The stress of the so-called "Operations Tempo" or OPTEMPO, of those days eventually led to congressional hearings in which I was selected to represent the Navy, a story told in later pages.

But all of that was in the future in the spring and summer of 1993, which is when this memoir begins. As this *Journal of a First Command* opens, a young commander is undergoing firefighting training in Newport, Rhode Island, with his classmates and friends, who are also en route to command at sea. It seems a long time ago.

Today, in the spring of 2007, as I write this preface some fourteen years later, I am wearing the four stars of a full admiral, and I lead a joint command with thousands of Soldiers, Sailors, Airmen, and Marines spread across the thirty-two countries and fifteen territories of the Caribbean and Central and South America. Headquartered in Miami, Florida, I command the U.S. Southern Command, reporting directly to the secretary of defense and the president. It is a long way from a commander's silver oak leaves and life on the USS *Barry*.

Indeed, my life in my fifties has moved on in ways I truly would have thought unimaginable in my thirties and seems so much more complicated, as is the case for most of us. Yet, I find that the occasionally uncertain and certainly unguarded voice of the young commander in this brief memoir still evokes for me both the best of times and the greatest of challenges in my life and lies at the heart of what I have learned and understand today about leadership and what is so aptly known as the call of the sea. I publish it in the hope that it will shed some small amount of light for the public on what it means to be lucky enough to command a U.S. warship at sea and to share, if only for a moment, the occasional doubts and small victories of a young officer sailing the world's seas in the turbulent closing days of the twentieth century.

I

The fire exploded in my face. I dragged the heavy nozzle of the fire hose toward the flames and pointed the solid stream of water toward the base of the fire.

For a long moment, the water had no effect. Then, as the sweat poured down my face inside the stifling oxygen-breathing apparatus, the flames flickered, seemed to sputter as the water continued to pour over them, and suddenly died, changing to a heavy blanket of steam, choking and hot, filling the tiny space.

I backed the hose team out of the small, brick-lined enclosure and turned to face my fellow firefighting trainees, five of whom had been backing me up during my turn as the nozzleman, leading the charge at the fire. We breathed a collective sigh of relief and pulled off our masks.

The faces that emerged from the masks were of men in their late thirties and early forties—faces just beginning to show the deepening concerns and cares of age, the sense of maturity that settles into the faces of people moving slowly but reasonably successfully along the carefully orchestrated career pattern of a military officer.

And each face showed the characteristic lines around the eyes common to Sailors who spend long hours staring at the distant horizon of the sea.

Each face belonged to a man who was going to command a U.S. Navy ship.

Three friends in particular were manning the hose with me that day. Each, I suspected, would go far in this Navy, probably a good deal farther than me. Cdr. Denis Army, a New Englander headed to command a *Spruance*-class destroyer, the USS *Arthur W. Radford*, was a big, good-natured, and outgoing officer who also anchored our excellent class softball team. A superb natural athlete, Denis turned down an offer to play professional baseball after graduating from college to accept a commission and head to sea.

The other two were both classmates of mine from Annapolis, Mike Lefever and Roy Balaconis. Roy was a short (e.g., my height, about five feet six inches), pugnacious Bostonian and a former brigade boxing champion at the Naval Academy, where he was a leader in the class of 1976 in both friends and demerits. Roy would become the first captain of the new *Arleigh Burke*–class destroyer, the USS *Mitscher*.

Mike Lefever was among my very closest friends on active duty, a natural leader and upbeat officer with a sunny disposition and an easy laugh, who was headed to command a *Spruance*-class destroyer in Charleston.

All three were among the top officers I had met in my sixteen years in the Navy, and I suspected each had a legitimate shot at flag rank. Each was as excited as I about heading off to command a warship.

In my case, the ship was a destroyer, the USS *Barry*, a new *Arleigh Burke*–class warship carrying the complex Aegis combat system and a crew of 340 men.

This is my journal, begun that day after finishing firefighting class, designed to provide a periodic account of what is currently scheduled to be a two-year tour of duty in command of a warship, beginning on 21 October 1993, and scheduled through two years to roughly the fall of 1995.

2

Why keep a journal at all?

Let me begin with the simplest thing I understand about myself. I must go and do this thing, command a ship. It is a challenge that has called to me since my days at Annapolis in the early 1970s, beginning a bit after my arrival at the Academy in 1972.

When I initially arrived at Annapolis, strangely, given how things turned out, I wanted to become a Marine officer, as my father had been. But that first summer cruise, on a sleek cruiser named the USS *Jouett*, changed my view. From the time I walked to the bridge of a warship, I began to think about taking command of one and joining the long line of Sailors who led a ship to sea.

And along with the desire to command a ship, the other constant in my years in the Navy has been writing. I have always liked reading and writing and have published many professional articles and edited three books. I do it because I like to write; essentially, I like to participate in what nineteenth-century writers called "the great conversation."

I also learn by writing—about my subject, about myself, and about my profession.

Whether anyone else ever reads this doesn't matter to me.

But at the end of two years in command, I will have something more than the traditional ship's plaque and gift presented to a departing commanding officer.

I will have a periodic record of what was important and how I have felt about the experience, a resource that can remind me of what was done well and what was done badly, and a record—for myself—of my days in a niche of the profession that carries history, challenge, hard work, romance, and, I hope, at the end of the day, a sense of quiet accomplishment.

3

I remember as a midshipman, in my final summer at Annapolis, going to sea on a two-month training cruise on the newly commissioned aircraft carrier, the USS *Nimitz*. An enormous and powerful warship of nearly one hundred thousand tons and over a thousand feet in length, with nuclear propulsion, a crew of five thousand men, and an airwing of tremendous capability.

I stood eight hours of watch each day, worked another eight as an assistant division officer, and spent what little free time I had wandering the vast city-at-sea, trying to learn about this Navy I was about to enter.

It was an exhausting time.

And I remember one night waking up just after 0300, preparing to go on watch on the bridge, looking at my tired, unshaven, twenty-year-old face in the mirror, illuminated by the red lights of the compartment—designed to preserve night vision. I looked at the gaunt, tired-beyond-its-years face, and thought ahead to a career in the Navy.

I asked myself, first in my mind, then aloud, "What am I doing here? And who am I?"

So, before I talk about the thirty-eight-year-old man who seventeen years later is preparing to assume command of a destroyer, let me try and answer those questions that escaped me that night in 1972, on the supercarrier, at sea in the Caribbean.

My father was a Marine officer, and I grew up on military bases both in the United States and abroad. I loved to travel, to experience constantly the change and the challenge of new places, new friends, new ideas. The longest I have ever had the same address was while I was a midshipman at Annapolis— neither before nor since have I ever lived in the same place longer than three years, generally moving every year or two.

From my mother I inherited a love of books and reading; from my father a love of the service and our country. Annapolis was the logical place for an education, and I did reasonably well. I finished near the top of my class, played on the varsity squash and tennis teams, served as a brigade officer, and edited the Academy's major midshipman publication. I can't say I loved the Academy, but in all fairness, it prepared me well for the life I've undertaken in the seventeen years since graduating, much of it spent under way.

After Annapolis, I served at sea in a variety of cruisers and destroyers, as well as an engineer on an aircraft carrier, the tired and venerable USS *Forrestal*. I also worked ashore in Washington, D.C., on the chief of naval operations' and the secretary of the Navy's staffs. The Navy sent me to graduate school in international relations in Boston, where I earned a PhD from Tufts University, as well as to the National War College in Washington, D.C.

In 1992 I was "slated" (essentially assigned as the relief for the commanding officer) to the USS *Barry*, a newly commissioned destroyer. I had originally been slated to command a *Spruance*-class destroyer, but the first commanding officer of the *Barry*, Gary Roughead, had been selected a year early for the rank of captain, which opened the *Barry* up and made the timing right for me.

I began the eight months of training in March of 1993, a long "pipeline" of schools that included refresher education in shiphandling, engineering, tactics, firefighting and associated shipboard damage control, personnel management, leadership, and countless other subjects.

The past in prologue.

So let me describe, briefly, the eight months of pipeline training.

4

After seventeen years in the Navy and thousands of days at sea, why do we need to send our prospective commanding officers through another eight months of schools?

I have thought long about this question.

And I don't have a very good answer, other than the most obvious one—because some of them need it.

Of course, not all of them need all of the training. Obviously, the better approach would be ascertaining who—among the dozens of prospective commanding officers who matriculate through the pipeline annually—needs what portion of the training. We could then provide a sort of precision-guided training to each officer to bring him or her up to speed as necessary in given subjects.

The Navy doesn't work that way, however.

We instead establish a baseline of knowledge that every commanding officer should have been exposed to over his or her career and then send everyone through a refresher that covers all that material.

It is, admittedly, a conservative and lowest-common-denominator approach. It can be maddening to sit through endless lectures about subjects in which you are already quite proficient, at least in your own mind. Yet, I suppose in the long run, it makes good sense—primarily because of the unique and difficult challenges we place before our commanding officers.

The pipeline for an Aegis-class ship CO is quite long because of the various specific combat systems schools involved. Mine began in mid-March of 1993 with a couple of days of Tomahawk missile school, teaching me the details on the lethal, precision-guided, long-range (750 mile plus) land-attack weapon. I was plunged into a seemingly interminable engineering school that walked me in detail through the entire complex gas-turbine engineering complex over the course of the next three months. By mid-June, we had taken a "field trip" from the course location in Newport, Rhode Island, up to Great Lakes, Illinois, where, in between drinking beer and eating bratwurst, we "traced" the engineering pipes through a mock-up of the entire engineering plant, which is the term the Navy uses for the entire complex of machines and rooms that constitute the propulsion system of a ship. It was hot, hard work in early summer.

This was followed in June and July in Newport with the actual Prospective Commanding Officer course, which focused on shiphandling, tactics, international law, leadership, safety, communications, and a myriad of other things over a fast-paced six weeks. The highlight of this period was our class's excellent softball team, which went 23-2. It was anchored by Denis Army, an amazing athlete and semipro baseball player, who, from the shortstop position, managed to cover essentially the entire infield and short field. I was at second base, which allowed Denis to cover my shortcomings nicely, and Roy Balaconis, an excellent hitter and fielder, was in left. My close friend, Mike Lefever, was our third baseman, and between him, Denis, and me, we could shut down almost everything hit on the ground. Summer softball, fueled by plenty of beer, is really a defensive game, and we came out on top frequently. It was an enjoyable time, far better than the three-month grind of engineering that had preceded it.

In the fall, I spent a month at Aegis school in Dahlgren, Virginia. The Aegis combat system is the most capable warfighting package ever put to sea. It can effectively fight the ship in all dimensions—against air targets most notably, but also very capably against subsurface and surface targets. It encompasses sensors, displays, weapons, and man-machine interfaces, and it has a great deal of helpful automatic response ability built into the suite. Dahlgren is a very rural area near the Rappahanock River, and as I was there without family—Laura and the girls were still in Washington, D.C., preparing to move to Norfolk—I spent the time playing tennis, running, and doing the minimal amount of studying necessary. Having served previously on two other Aegis-class ships, I felt—probably incorrectly—that I knew most of what the class had to offer.

After Dahlgren, I attended a couple more short courses. Then I plowed through three weeks of relatively complex tactics in Virginia Beach and at the Dam Neck complex. This course, the tactical training portion of the pipeline, was excellent. It was taught by relatively senior officers who had recent command and seagoing experience. If the entire nine months of pipeline could be boiled down, this was what I thought should be the heart of the course.

After the long nine months, I was ready—more than ready—to set foot on the deck of a ship again. So, off to Norfolk I went, moved the family into a nice house on the water in Little Neck, and prepared for the week-long turnover on the *Barry*.

5

Taking command begins with something we in the Navy call simply "turnover." It is a generally brief (five-to-seven-day) period over the course of which two naval officers change their lives significantly. One, after two years in command, is providing his or her relief with a detailed view of the ship. The other, after waiting seventeen or eighteen years in the Navy, is assuming command—and responsibility and accountability—for a ship. It is a stressful time for both naval officers directly involved, as well as for the ship and crew being passed along.

In my case, I walked aboard the *Barry* on the morning of 12 October 1993. She was moored port side to the pier, at Pier 24 of the Norfolk naval station, at one of the outboard berths.

I parked my car in a designated space and walked slowly up the pier. As I walked, carrying three small overnight bags, a young petty officer approached me and recognized who I was.

He asked if I wanted any help with my bags and welcomed me aboard. I carried my own bags, thinking it poor form to start the tour asking for personal help.

As I walked along the pier, a snippet from Patrick O'Brian's superb book about the nineteenth-century Royal Navy was running through my head. In *Master and Commander*, the first book of the series, a young British naval officer is about to take command of his first ship. He thinks to himself, "I felt a curious shortness of breath, for my heart was beating high, and I had difficulty in swallowing. Am I afraid? he wondered." I felt exactly the same thing walking the pier on that sunny fall morning in Norfolk.

The incumbent commanding officer, Capt. Gary Roughead, met me at the top of the gangplank.

A superb officer, Roughead had been a brigade commander at Annapolis with the class of 1973—three years senior to me. He had been early selected promotion several times and had a reputation as a very competent, low-key leader who had put together a superb team in the *Barry*. Tall and gracious, he looked every inch the admiral I was sure he would become. He towered over me, a picture of confidence that I wished I felt. He was a man in full, at the end of a successful run in command, and had an excellent service reputation to boot. As I was to discover over the next four days, it was a reputation richly deserved.

6

As I first walked across the broad fantail of the *Arleigh Burke*–class destroyer, the *Barry*, I was struck by the smiles of the crew members. In fact, throughout the next four days, I seldom saw a crew member who did not, upon seeing me, smile and welcome me aboard.

The ship was scrupulously clean, the spaces well painted and well preserved, and the *ship ran on time*, so to speak.

The executive officer, an old friend of mine, was Cdr. Charlie Martoglio, with whom I had crossed paths both in the fleet and in Washington, D.C. His continuing friendliness, competence, and evident concern for his ship was immediately apparent.

Events seemed to accelerate almost instantly. After dropping my gear off in a small cabin assigned for my use during the turnover week, I walked into the crowded bridge, where the sea detail—the full-manning used to get the ship ready to head to sea—was already set. I walked over to Gary Roughead and tried to stay out of his way as he worked with his team to prepare to get the ship under way.

The wind was blowing hard (thirty knots) down the pier, and a strong ebb current was evident out in the channel. It was clearly going to be a bit challenging getting her under way. While I was a confident shiphandler, I had never had the opportunity to "drive" one of these new *Arleigh Burke*–class ships, which had already developed a reputation as fine sea-keepers—excellent to handle in an open seaway but difficult around the pier.

The pilot was a bit late. The steering was not responding well, and the under way—scheduled for 0830—was delayed about twenty minutes. I could see Gary's frustration, but as always, he handled it calmly as the team worked through the various procedures to bring the systems up to the mark. Finally, both tugs were pulling us out toward the center of the narrow slip. We drove ahead into the channel, threw a full rudder on the ship, and headed fair out the channel toward the windy Chesapeake Bay.

Over the next four nights, Gary Roughead and his team put the ship through virtually all of her paces. Guns were fired, damage control drills were executed, engineering casualties were corrected, man overboard shiphandling drills were conducted, aircraft were tracked through the unseasonably cold skies of the Virginia coast. Through it all, it was clear that the wardroom was competent and well led by Gary and Charlie, although to my eye, the long, stressful precommissioning period had clearly taken its toll on the group. In casual conversations with many of the younger officers, I found that it did not seem that many intended on staying in the Navy for a career, a somewhat surprising discovery on a brand-new ship with a solid CO and executive officer (XO). To all of that, I mentally shrugged my shoulders when I reviewed the document that showed the timeline of all the officers—virtually all of the commissioning wardroom would be gone over the next six months, and I would be working with my own team quite shortly. Even the superb XO, Charlie Martoglio, would depart within a few months. So, for better or worse, the team I would have in the *Barry*, at least in the wardroom, would be like me—new to the ship.

The chiefs' mess, in a word, was superb. I had never met a better team, ably led by a relatively newly appointed command master chief, Stan Brown. Their confidence and depth were immediately evident, and, unlike the wardroom, virtually all of them would be remaining for at least a year or two beyond my arrival.

So, on balance, as I watched the ship work through a full agenda of turnover training, I felt quite pleased with the hand I'd been dealt. As we set a course for Norfolk late on a Wednesday night before a Friday change of command, I went to sleep feeling as ready as I could be to take the captain's chair, if still a bit nervous of what lay ahead.

7

Change of command day, early in the morning hours. I am nursing a bad flu, which has left me dizzy and exhausted. I'm loaded up on decongestants, which are slowly drying out my inner ear and making the dizziness recede. As I pull on my blues, I look in the mirror and feel old, old, old. I'm thirty-eight years of age, and my eyes look tired. Can I really handle this?

8

My parents, my wife's parents, my sister, and our niece are the "headliner" guests. Some special friends make the trek to distant Norfolk on this sunny, windy, and mild fall afternoon—Al Fraser, John Morgan, and Kevin Green, all of whom will be flag officers someday, I believe.

Al Fraser, a full captain on his way to cruiser command, and his wife, Sheila, are among my oldest friends. Al was a few years ahead of me at Annapolis, and as a young married couple, Sheila and Al took me under their wing when I first arrived in San Diego as a very green ensign in 1976. We'd been close friends ever since, including three years when Al and I served together in the USS *Valley Forge*. Al had been the executive officer in *Valley Forge*, and I was operations officer, working for him and Capt. Ted Lockhart.

John Morgan, a newly minted captain, was likewise a friend of many years standing and had been the commissioning commanding officer in the USS *Arleigh Burke*, the lead ship of the class. He had been particularly kind to me when I was in the pipeline, making the *Arleigh Burke* available for tours and visits during the long months of my training before the *Barry* came to Norfolk. He had just been selected for another sea command, this time of a squadron of destroyers.

And finally, Kevin Green, also a relatively junior captain, but like John Morgan, having already been selected for assignment as a commodore at sea. Kevin had been a classmate of mine at the National War College a couple of years earlier.

All three of them were people I looked up to in very real ways. As I saw them sitting at the change of command, each having successfully completed command at sea, I hoped I wouldn't disappoint them or their hopes for my success.

The ceremony itself was quite pleasant, as such things often are, and the reception afterward was enjoyable as well. So many people, piling on so many wishes and hopes for your future—it makes you feel at once happy to have such good friends around and also so aware of the expectations and hopes they have. But it was all over by the middle of the day, and finally, as I drove home to our house after a celebratory dinner at a Greek restaurant, it hit me—I was the captain. No matter how it all turned out, I had taken my place, uncertain though it felt in that moment, as part of a profession stretching back through time for centuries and centuries. Not a bad moment. Not bad at all.

9

The first day of work as "The Captain" begins at a relatively leisurely hour for the military culture. I walk across the brow to four bells and "*Barry*, arriving," at 0810. The crew has been at work for about an hour.

Why the relatively late arrival?

Because once the captain is aboard, there is a greater tendency to brief me, to slow work and come by to let me know about things—far better to arrive a bit later and let the executive officer get the day started.

My XO, Charlie Martoglio, opens the door to my cabin. We sit and he begins the first of some seven hundred plus days I hope to spend in command.

Today's crises open fast—a crew member is in sick bay threatening to kill himself; another has been crushed by news of his wife's affair and is requesting transfer ashore to try and sort things out; we will be hosting the deputy secretary of defense in four days; the ship has been selected to sail to Haiti in ten day's time for at least two months of contingency operations; problems with the ammo load needed for the coming Haitian contingency operations. The list goes on and on.

I sit taking this in, still feeling terrible.

The flu and dizziness that have plagued me all week resurfaced over the weekend, the result, no doubt, of drinking, dancing, celebrating, and running endless errands to support all of the guests attending the change of command.

I feel tired and full of doubt.

After the XO's litany, he departs, and I sip bitter coffee the messman has brought in. Here it is, Jim, the best tour of your life. If only the room would stop spinning.

Slowly, I start trying to put away files and prepare for the day ahead.

10

More on the first day in command: I walk the ship, meeting people, trying to find my way to places I am still unsure of. Does this door lead to the combat information center or the career counselor's office? How stupid can I look?

I see a petty officer—a radioman, a signalman, or a boatswain's mate. Have I met him before?

But at least I'm fulfilling one key goal I've always had— to be out and about in the ship at least half of my time.

II

My second day in command is much better. The best part is
that the virus seems to be passing and the dizziness is gone. I
am slightly drowsy from the decongestant, and my right knee
is still tender.

Otherwise, a far better day.

I feel I am starting to make a contribution, making some
decisions and helping get things accomplished.

I pay a call on the commodore, a fatherly figure of about
my stature. We talk about racquetball, the running of ships,
and taking care of the crew. His chief staff officer is energetic
and pleasant and helps arrange a smooth move for the ship
on Wednesday.

I meet with other members of the destroyer squadron
staff, and they are all helpful and bright and seem very young
to me. It does occur to me that much of my future in the Navy
will be bound up in how my ship—and therefore I, as the
captain—is viewed at the destroyer squadron headquarters. I
am not one to overthink the issue of fitness reports, the annual
evaluation that all officers in the Navy receive, but I would
not be human if I didn't occasionally hope that I will receive
a strong report. If I do, two things will happen: First, and
most important, it will be a validation of all my work on the
ship and a way to measure how well I am leading my Sailors.
Second, it will be the gateway to another command at sea.
Both, I think are good things. But clearly, all I can do is try
my best, not worry about how the paper turns out, follow my
inner compass, and hope for the best.

Later that same day, I call the Commander of Surface
Forces in the Atlantic Fleet staff, my boss's boss, to try to
arrange for a remote thermal imager sight to help in the
coming Haitian operations. It may be a successful effort.
Time will tell. I probably shouldn't be "going around" my
immediate boss, but I rationalize doing so to myself by saying
I'm pushing for the right thing for my ship and time is of

the essence. Hopefully, my engagement will help. Having a thermal imager will be very helpful in identifying contacts at night and accomplishing our mission in the Caribbean, which will be to interdict contraband from coming into that troubled island.

Likewise, I "weigh in" on obtaining new shore-power breakers and a magnetic-flux compass (sort of a high-tech magnetic compass). Again, I am paid lip service, but within a few days I will know how it turns out. It's hard to say how much making such calls helps, but it seems to me that's a basic part of my job—advocating and pushing the system to equip my ship fully for her coming mission.

I am certainly enjoying working with the command master chief, Stan Brown, an ex-trucker, biker, forester, firefighter turned Navy master chief. An interesting and capable man. The command master chief on a ship is the senior enlisted man or woman, and their job is to act as an interface between the commanding officer and the crew. Sometimes—infrequently, really—they are merely decorative, and at other times, they can counterproductively act as a sort of aggressive "shop steward" for the crew. Most often, in my experience, they are exceptional leaders from whom young captains like me can certainly learn a good deal. Stan Brown is absolutely in the latter category. He has a nice touch with the Sailors—both friendly but with a clear edge of "tough love" and a sincere and honest tone in helping guide me through our first few issues. I know instinctively we'll be a good team and that I'll learn a lot from him.

Clearly emerging as a star in this wardroom is the supply officer, Lt. Tim Morgan. Because of the coming and relatively short-notice deployment to Haiti, I ask him if he wants to cancel or postpone his big annual supply inspection—a chance at which most if not all of his contemporaries would jump—and he emphatically wants to take the inspection. When I tell him I think I can get it pushed off or even waived, he says simply, "Captain, we're ready to go, and I want my team to have a chance to show how good they are. Let us take the inspection. We won't let you or the ship down." With an attitude like that, there's no answer but go to it.

12 *In Command a Week*

We are deep in the throes of preparing to depart for two months off the coast of Haiti, responding to national-level tasking and the growing instability in Hispanola. We will be conducting maritime interception operations in support of UN policy—Operation Restore Democracy is the U.S. equivalent operation. We evidently will be working under a U.S. Navy chain of command, and I think one of the senior officers afloat down there will be Capt. Mike Mullen, one of my idols. I have known Mike since my days as a midshipman, when he was a company officer at Annapolis. He is currently in command of an Aegis-class cruiser, the *Yorktown*, and rumor has it he will be the senior officer afloat and will be in charge. I hope so. You couldn't ask for a better or more steady boss at sea than Mike Mullen.

I've been pushing the crew and the wardroom hard. This is an unannounced deployment, and the ship is really just out of the building yards. But I sense we can do a good job down there if we get ourselves ready. That means a full and complete load out of ammo, food, fuel. Perhaps most important, we must all get our family situations under control, briefing the wives, ensuring everyone has a correct contact path to get information, wills are updated, powers of attorney provided, and a thousand other things. The families are acutely aware we'll be deploying for a full six months in the spring of next year, so this two-month "Haitian vacation," as it is being called on the mess decks, is not being met with much enthusiasm on the home front. Here on the ship, however, it's a different story. I feel a sense in the crew that they want to get out and do their thing in a real-world crisis. I just hope I'm ready to do what I need to do. At times, it feels very real and a bit intimidating, going to sea with 340 people, all looking to me for leadership. It would have been nice to have a few "day trips," so to speak, but that just isn't the way it's played out.

In the midst of all this, we do what the Navy so often sends along to an already too busy ship and crew: we host a VIP tour. It will be composed of the deputy secretary of defense, Dr. Bill Perry, a noted technologist, and full four-star admiral Hank Mauz, the commander of the Atlantic Fleet. They will be on board for just one hour. I spend the night before the visit working on my Aegis knowledge, cramming like the graduate student I once was. I am absolutely convinced that Doctor Perry, a brilliant scientist, will ask me a series of incredibly technical questions and embarrass me in front of my fleet commander.

As with all VIP tours, they came and went.

Fortunately, the deputy secretary of defense doesn't seem to know all that much about Aegis—or frankly a heck of a lot about ships, for that matter. But he is clearly very intelligent and listens carefully to everything we tell him. Fortunately for me, he is also a real gentlemen, who goes out of his way to be kind, friendly, and encouraging to my crew. The tour goes very well, and Admiral Mauz focuses the secretary on Theater Ballistic Missile Defense (TBMD). Despite my doubts, all seems to go well, and I am congratulated on the impressiveness of my ship.

13

The rest of the week and the weekend pass in a blur. The fact that I will leave for Haiti on Wednesday still isn't sinking in, although the preparations continue to accelerate. We load in a good deal of tactical (reed explosive) ammunition for the 5-inch gun—a good weapon for gunboat diplomacy, I suppose. Actually, I'd say the odds of using the heavy weapons are quite slim—fortunately. I'm really worried about the ability of my boarding team—a group of Sailors trained to go over to other ships and inspect them—because that will be "the main battery" on this little excursion.

Mostly, we are pulling stores aboard—FFV (fresh vegetables and fruit); electronic components for our complex display systems in the combat information center; UDT milk, which is boxed, has an indefinite shelf life, and resembles milk only a little; countless cases of sodas, which the thirsty Sailors will suck down endlessly in the hot Caribbean; nonalcoholic beer for "steel beach" cookouts; fishing poles and skeet-shooting rigs; turkeys for Thanksgiving; and the thousand other things that will make life somewhat palatable at sea.

This is a busy but good time.

I think that, throughout the long, long, long history of man and ships, there have been scenes exactly like this, as Phoenician sailors and Vikings and Romans and the Spanish Armada and Nelson's HMS *Victory*, and every other ship in history scurried to load aboard what it needed for the coming voyage.

14

It is the Monday before we sail. I've given the crew the day off to allow them time to prepare their homes, cars, and families for the sudden two-month cruise.

I come to the quiet ship. We are pulling the last few cases of supplies for the ship's store—potato chips, canned iced tea, underwear, black socks—and a few final pallets of naval gunfire ammunition. Quite a contrast—black socks for my Sailors and the heavy 5-inch gun projectiles that may end up hurtling thirteen miles over the pounding surf and into the coast of distant Haiti. I hope it doesn't come to that. The only scenario I can imagine that would have us shooting in anger at the Haitian coast would be a NEO (noncombatant evacuation operation), which would result only from attacks on Americans.

Hard to imagine General Raoul Cedras being that stupid. On the other hand, the whole thing is starting to remind me of Panama, which General Manuel Noriega started by harassing Americans—notably an Army officer and his wife—and President George H. W. Bush simply stepped in and took over the country. I hope the president doesn't find that necessary. Hopefully, diplomacy, the United Nations, and a flotilla of ships will make all of that unnecessary.

On the ship, I read some message traffic, notably a personal message from the captain of the *Connolly*, a *Spruance*-class destroyer on station and a fellow *George Washington* battle group member. I also picked a plaque style for the ship's store, walked through the engineering spaces, worked on crew welfare with the command master chief (library, magazines, sporting goods), talked to the supply officer about the final load of stores; and called my boss, the commodore, to tell him our preparations for sailing were coming along very well.

Then I hopped in the Volvo and drove home through the sunny, crisp fall in Norfolk, Virginia, still waiting for the reality of a six-week separation from Laura and my two daughters to hit me.

As I pull into the driveway and looked through the lighted kitchen window, I can see my beautiful blonde wife, Laura, at the sink. Daughter of a Navy captain, she knows the drill. She'll be "at the conn," as we say in the Navy—in charge of our two little daughters, eight and three, for the two months. Then for the full six months. Before this two-year tour is over, I'll be gone for eighteen months of it, I'd guess. God, I'll miss her every day. She is the nicest person I've ever met.

15

The night before a long under way is always hard.

I took my eight-year-old daughter out to dinner at Chili's and had a wonderful time talking with her about school and grades and gymnastics and her new school—Kingston Elementary—which is why we moved to the area we did. I heard all the things that run through an eight-year-old's mind.

Then home, and Laura and I worked on putting Julia, our three year old, to bed and on Christina's homework.

I packed, we went to bed, and before long, the morning was upon me. All night long, I kept thinking of them, then of the ship, then of them, then of the ship. What on earth am I doing?

Laura and the girls—all of them, a real treat—drove me to the ship, I kissed them good-bye, and then I turned my face to the ship and prepared to go to sea.

16

We sailed this morning for Haiti.

What can you say about the first under way as a new commanding officer?

I was nervous. All morning, I kept thinking ahead to the various commands that would move my beautiful, nine-thousand-ton destroyer off the pier. We were moored port side to Pier 25, and I mentally walked through the orders that would launch us toward Haiti—make up the tugs, single up all lines, take in all lines, all back on both tugs, all ahead one third, right full rudder—and all the countless permutations and possible combinations of wind and current and tide that might affect the under way.

At 0930 the pilot arrived—an older, experienced gentleman, one of the pilots Gary Roughead had pointed out as a good one. He made up two tugs fore and aft, and we agreed he would simply pull us straight back, drop off the after tug, and let us go forward smoothly. It was an easy and low-risk under way, just the kind I liked. There would be plenty of time later in the tour to do some "fancy shiphandling," which I was looking forward to. But at this moment, I thought, let's just get out of here in one piece.

The conning officer was the damage control assistant, Lt. Brandon Kot. He was an experienced officer, and I felt sure he wouldn't need a great deal of guidance.

At about 0945, I ordered the lines taken in, the brow lifted, and the tugs to start pulling us off the pier. It was a cold and windy morning, with a media van on the pier and perhaps a dozen wives and girlfriends waving. The wind was blowing at perhaps twenty knots from the southwest, and the river was running with about a knot and a half of flood tide.

It all went smoothly, and the ship quickly moved into the channel and pointed fair toward the sea.

The transit out of the naval base was smooth and relatively uneventful. The only moment of interest was as the ship turned the corner north of the naval station. The current hit us broadside and pushed the ship sharply to the left of the channel. So we moved to the right quite smartly to correct. I had to jump into the process myself, which was fine. As a general proposition, I had decided I wanted to let the young officers drive the ship and make a few mistakes, as long as the ship wasn't endangered. I thought of myself as a good shiphandler and had written a few articles about it. But I also know that I'm far from infallible, and it seems to me the trick is in knowing when to jump into the problem and correct something before it gets too far out of hand. I've always loved the quote from Adm. Ernest King, perhaps the most eccentric CNO the Navy has ever experienced, who said, "The best ship handling is comprised of never getting in a situation that requires exceptional ship handling." In other words, take the conservative path, don't let your ego drive the ship, and take advantage of assistance—like tugs and a pilot—when available. I never forget that the pilot who walks aboard my ship to help us get under way has done more in-close shiphandling that month than I'll do in my entire career.

Within three hours, we were in the open ocean and moving south smoothly, headed fair toward the island of Hispanola and the maritime interdiction operation around the nation of Haiti.

17 *A Good Day at Sea*

Woke up to a beautiful morning, calm glass seas, and warm sunny air.

We worked the boarding team hard. Led by Lt. Terry Mosher, our weapons officer, the boarding team consists of twelve outstanding petty officers and Ens. Dave Demarcyk, our electronic material officer and a limited duty officer (former enlisted man). Terry is the kind of innovative, intuitive officer who can take a commercial "off the shelf" computer program and create a homemade training program for the entire ship. He crackles with intellectual energy and always has a good idea about what we should try next. Dave Demarcyk is one of the funniest members of our wardroom, a slender, energetic and very social fellow—someone you'd like to have at your side in a bar. You can see the inner pirate struggling to get out. He'll end up running a saloon in Key West some day, I'll bet.

I went for a run around the decks at lunch, helped in training the boarding team after lunch, and attended a series of briefings about the coming maritime interception operations.

The crew's mood seems upbeat and ready for real-world action.

Tonight I'm watching the movie *Unforgiven*, with Clint Eastwood, Gene Hackman, and Morgan Freeman. An interesting, seemingly realistic view of the late 1800s western. But, like the difference between the Navy of the movies and the real Navy, the difference between *Unforgiven* and the real West is actually quite sharp, I suspect.

I'm also reading a little. At the moment, I'm dipping lightly into two great sea novels, *The Cruel Sea* by Nicholas Monsarrat and *The Good Shepherd* by C. S. Forester. Both wonderful reads and good stories for the captain. My plan during this tour is to read through the fifteen or so novels by Patrick O'Brian, which center on a British naval captain at the turn of the nineteenth century, Jack Aubrey, and his odd, but brilliant ship's surgeon, Stephen Maturin. I've read the first of the series, *Master and Commander,* and found it quite a good meditation on command at sea. Others who have worked through the entire series tell me that it is vastly better than C. S. Forester's Hornblower series, which I find quite good. So, I'm very hopeful of O'Brian. My goal is to spend lots of time on my chair in the pilot house or on the bridge wing, reading a good novel—I think it's important to show the younger folk that (a) reading matters and, more important, that (b) it is a good deal being the captain. If I can't communicate the joy of command to my wardroom, why would any of them want to stick around? It sure isn't for the pay!

18

Today we arrived off the coast of Haiti.

We had ourselves a long night steam down the Florida coast, a beautiful dawn trip by San Salvador, and a quick transit through the Crooked Island Passage, past the point where Christopher Columbus found the New World. As we pass through the passage, I jump on the 1MC, the ship's announcing system, and provide a little color commentary. I think it is fun for the crew to take a quick break from wherever they are in this big steel hull and come up on deck to see what we pass that is interesting. I am going to keep doing it and see how they like it over time. The trick is not to be tiresome, but rather to jump on and off quickly. After all, one of the big benefits of life at sea is having an office with a great view, right?

Think of it. This is a part of the world through which flowed all the treasure of the New World, carried in Spanish galleons back to the waiting king and queen—and often preyed upon by the English, the Dutch, and many other adventurers. Beneath the *Barry*'s wide, smooth hull are the ruins of a hundred old sailing ships, vessels on a long voyage to eternity.

I find myself looking at the sea and sky quite a bit here in the Caribbean in the early days of this two-year command. And I feel, surrounding me in every cloud and deep blue sky, a sense of being part of a world that has stretched on forever. You truly can feel eternity out here. It is everywhere at sea, in the sky and the ocean and the clouds. Eternity.

I see it as well in the faces of my daughters, in the smile of my wife in the pictures on my desk. God I miss them, and we've only been gone a few days. This will be a long tour.

19 *Haiti*

A barren island when seen through binoculars, yet curiously tropical when seen from a distance. The Haitians have, for a generation, been burning their trees into charcoal for a cheap source of fuel. Now the island is almost literally washing away.

We steamed through the Windward Passage early this morning after enjoying a gorgeous tropical sunset.

The island has a rich and generally harsh history: settled by the French, the scene of numerous slave uprisings and unbelievably harsh reprisals. Its Creole language is almost unrecognizable as a French derivative, and its Voodoo religion is among the world's oddest, at least to one raised in the Christian tradition. But in reading about the island, you develop a certain respect for the toughness of the people and the challenges of their lives. I doubt we'll go ashore, although I'd be fascinated to. So, as is so often the case for Sailors, I'll float along the coast, idly observing through binoculars, reading and learning about the culture, then probably sailing away to the next assignment. There is such a transitory quality to the Sailor's life.

But back to work in the ship: A main-space fire drill, general quarters, then an easy Saturday afternoon for the ship. My sense is that we will be working hard over the next few weeks—so before we formally "check in" with the embargo commander, I thought it best to give the crew a few hours off.

We slowed the ship to dead slow; threw fishing lines over the fantail; served up some nonalcoholic beer, which was at least ice cold; and, in general, tried to have a relaxing afternoon. And I think we succeeded.

After a couple of hours fishing, back to business—we landed a helicopter, onloaded two Coast Guard officers for boarding officer training, and motored ahead slowly toward the coast of Haiti.

20 *Late the Same Night*

We have received a message tasking us to park overnight in the same "box" (a ten by ten nautical mile area off the Haitian coast) as a huge amphibious ship is parked. I have spoken with all my officers of the deck and asked them to be extraordinarily careful. Who knows? I have to sleep sometime, and all I can do is all I can do.

And so, how am I feeling? Pretty good, I guess. I have a harsh headache and a grumbling stomach, caused by a flu bug passing around the ship.

But I feel more confident each day—really each hour—in the ship. After the underway replenishment on Monday and a few more port calls, I think I'll start to relax.

It is going well with the crew. I am a novelty, after all. After three years with Gary—who is a wonderful and competent officer, to say the least—having a new captain makes a quite startling change for the crew. From what I can gather, I suppose I get out into the ship perhaps a bit more than he did—a reflection of all the good training he did to make the bridge and combat information teams so competent that I am comfortable doing so. But that does make a change for the crew, and in their own way, they comment on it. A few nice notes in the suggestion box, a few of the bolder ones making kind comments verbally. It is nothing more than the normal "honeymoon" afforded any reasonably outgoing new commanding officer. It will not last, I'm sure. But it is nice while it's here.

I remember a long time ago, when I went to sea on the enormous aircraft carrier the USS *Nimitz,* I was a very young midshipman first class. I stood bridge watches, oddly enough, in these same waters. That was almost twenty years ago, back in the summer of '75. And on one of those long midwatches, the JOOD, an already burning out lieutenant who seemed incredibly old to me then, said to me, "When I'm ashore, I never want to go to sea. And when I'm at sea, I never want to come ashore." There is a grain of truth in that when you sail in a good ship, in calm waters, doing something that means something, for a country you love.

And on that note, I'll go to bed—for the average of thirty minutes or so between phone calls thanks to the close presence of my amphibious neighbor. The officer of the deck (OOD) is required to call whenever there is a possibility of the ships approaching within five miles of each other. Which is roughly all the time in our small box. I need to register with the commodore out here that there must be a better way to spread the ships around the coast!

21

We did our first UNREP—underway replenishment—today, the *Barry* and I. The ship had done a few before, but I had not seen this during the turnover. It is an intricate, but not terribly difficult, bit of seamanship and shiphandling. It means that two huge ships, one an oiler with fuel, food, and/or ammunition to give, and the other a receiver, perhaps a destroyer like mine, steer close together on parallel courses, about 140 feet apart. Then, like two parallel trains running over invisible tracks in the ocean, the ships hook up with each other and the oil and stores pass across the ocean churning between. Scary the first time you see it. Eventually, it looks somewhat routine.

The seas were running a bit, with white caps and about fifteen knots of wind. The ship moved smoothly over the sea, and we pulled into station behind the large oiler, the USS *Henry Kaiser*. The XO had the conn, at my request, and did a superb job bringing the ship up and into station. We cut the engines and glided into station aside the oiler, and the lines passed swiftly between the two ships. It was a very warm—almost tropical—day, with flying fish bounding up between the ships.

We broke away at thirty knots, an accelerating mass of gray steel cutting through the dark blue Caribbean sea.

The tradition on Navy ships is to play a song on the 1MC announcing system when breaking away. I choose "The Heat Is On" from the Eddie Murphy movie, *Beverly Hills Cop*. Seemed to get a rise out of the crew, and I think I'll stay with it.

The rest of the day was spent with the tiresome business of querying merchant shipping, trying to determine who would require boarding and who could be given a pass through the Windward Passage, sailing free past the dark mass of Haiti.

Chicken gumbo for dinner and blueberry cheesecake for dessert; and I'm half watching *Grand Canyon*. It's not really all so bad, this thing we call sea duty. But I miss Laura.

22

I'm reading *The Cruel Sea* by Nicholas Monsarrat, for at least the fourth time in my life.

It has never held more meaning for me—the story of a young (in this case, very young, in his twenties) captain, working so hard to carry his ship, the demands of the sea, the long sleepless nights, the pressure and the stress and the strain. I am learning a great deal and appreciating my life more—especially my life ashore. Things are far easier today, in the way of creature comforts, at least. Yet, in other ways, they are remarkably like the British navy of the 1930s or the American Navy of the 1820s or any other navy that has ever sailed. At least for the ship's captain.

You are forever at the center of the maelstrom. No matter the calmness or storminess of the moment, you stand forever at the center.

There is a wonderful quote from that book, which I can never quite remember, but basically it goes like this:

The Captain carried them all.
For him, there was not set watch, nor any
established time to rest and retreat from the
harsh conditions of the sea.
He was wonderfully reliable, uncomplaining,
and ready to take any watch, no matter the hour
or the situation.
He was the kind of Captain to have.

God, I hope I'm that kind of captain. Time will tell.

23 *The Patrol Continues*

Haiti looms, malignant and slightly nonsensical, just over the horizon. The seas have picked up, perhaps to sea state four, with a significant chop and over twenty knots of wind blowing, although it is clear and beautiful and we can see all the way to the dusty foothills of old Hispaniola.

The ship motors along apace. Today's crisis was a very near disaster. A major fuel oil spill inside the module of number three gas turbine generator. A moment to explain: Our ship's electricity is generated by three large jet engines, which turn generators and power the ship. Today, one of the generators suffered a fuel spill inside the module that encases it. The potential for catastrophe in such situations is very high, because if the stream of pressurized fuel had hit a sufficiently hot engine component, a major fire could have resulted.

At a minimum, such a fire would knock out about a third of the ship's electrical capacity and destroy the expensive engine. This would necessitate pulling off station and steaming, with our figurative tail between our legs, into Puerto Rico for an engine repair.

At worst, should the fire have spread to the surrounding engine room, the ship itself could have been endangered by explosion, and, at the darkest side of the equation, by many deaths and great damage to the ship. It has happened at sea, and not long ago, in a *Spruance*-class destroyer.

Fortunately, that was not the case today.

An alert watch stander in the space saw the stream of fuel coming out of the generator and punched the generator off the line before the fuel-air mixture could explode. We were helped by the fact that the generator itself was quite cold, having been off the line since midmorning. We spent the rest of the day cleaning and sorting out what had happened—the normal problem—people rushing to do a job had not completely bolted down a pressurized fuel connector line between the fuel filter and the rest of the generator.

The sound you hear is a bullet whizzing by all our heads on good ship *Barry*.

Like I told my engineer, "Sometimes you are lucky and sometimes you are good. Today we were lucky. From now on we need to be good."

24

Another day, another UNREP. Again, the seas were relatively calm, the teams ready, and the entire evolution went very smoothly. I continue to be amazed at the sight of tens of thousands of tons of ships steaming along within 140 feet of each other, passing ammunition, supplies, and parts across the foaming water between.

It amazed me so many long years ago on my first ship, the destroyer, the USS *Hewitt,* when the ships would pull up. We would approach at 100 feet then (as opposed to 120 to 150 feet today), and the pure adrenaline rush of pulling in at night was almost enough to knock me over.

I remember my first CO, Ted Alexander, a great shiphandler and a giant of a man, at least six feet five inches, towering over me, helping me bring the ship into station. He was relieved by my second CO, Fritz Gaylord, a wonderful gentleman, Stanford graduate, smooth, polished—a true gem. I learned so much from both of them—from them all, really, all the commanding officers I have worked for—that I use every day.

I hope in some small way I can pass along the skills and tricks of this trade to the young officers in my wardroom, and to the chief petty officer, and, indeed, to the youngest Sailors in the ship.

Today continues, now that the UNREP is over, as a quiet Saturday at sea. A combat photography team is embarking, so perhaps we'll do an actual boarding soon. I hope so. Things are pretty slow so far, although there is always a rhythm in the mission of a ship at sea that generates its own kind of beauty, its own kind of imprimatur.

25 *Another Sunday at Sea*

From the King James Bible, "But they that wait upon the LORD shall renew *their* strength; they shall mount up with wings as eagles; they shall run, *and* not be weary; and they shall walk, and not be faint." Isaiah 40:31. Truly, a motto for the Navy, where we routinely work eighteen to twenty hours a day at sea, standing watch for eight to twelve, then working a full day on top. That quotation was given me by the captain in the USS *Antietam*, a superb Aegis-class cruiser, home ported in Long Beach, California, in the late 1980s. It was commanded by Capt. Larry Eddingfield, and I was lucky to be second in command. Larry was a religious person, and he eventually retired from the Navy after a successful career to become an Episcopal priest. He was a fine person, and I learned a great deal from him about spirituality, about patience, and about paying attention to details. Every time I see that quote, I think of him, and the *Antietam*, which was an amazingly successful ship, winning virtually every award in the Pacific Fleet in the long-ago days of 1991.

The *Barry*, for whatever reason, has not had a tradition of taking many days off at sea. I have always believed in taking Sunday at sea off—having a cookout if the weather is nice, letting people fish and sun, perhaps fly a kite. All is gray and routine at sea, even in the most exciting operations; while a nice sunny day in the Caribbean definitively is not. Thus, anything to break the routine becomes mandatory to keep people sharp and believing in themselves and what they do.

I must admit I have met some resistance from senior people on board about taking a day off at sea; but even the British navy, the harshest of taskmasters, takes Sunday off at sea; and even the British Sailors have a daily tot of rum or beer, which we deny ourselves. There are times when it is good to be captain and to make decisions like this. We'll take the day off!

The seas are running a little stronger than before, but still the sunny, bright days and the cool and only slightly tropical nights. It will be a change for this crew when we push north in a few weeks.

I feel sad and somewhat lonely tonight. I cannot say why. Perhaps I am a little tired. I received perhaps twenty telephone calls last night, between 2300 and 0600. All were legitimate issues to put before the captain: changes of course, new tasking from the admiral who drives us around, possible embargo runners. And by the morning, I am tired and drawn.

Will I last two years at this?

Yet, other things pick me up. The engineer who tells me today he will extend for the cruise, because he is enjoying the Navy again. The young antisubmarine officer who wants to back out of a mediocre job assignment and throw his hat in the ring for a frontline position as an admiral's aide. The young Sailor who tells me it won't mean anything coming from him, but that the whole ship is happy I'm in command. It is he who can never know how much it means to me from one so young and, I think, sincere—he has nothing to gain from me as captain. I am as distant from him as the moon or the stars. But he stops me to tell me this.

Is it the normal "honeymoon" period enjoyed by any superior taking over an organization? Of course it is. But I do sincerely care for each of them. It is a task of service we set before our captains. Not all, sadly, grasp that. I learned it myself, late in the game, as an executive officer from Larry Eddingfield, my last commanding officer in the *Antietam*—command as service. Nothing is more important.

For no one is the term service more applicable than the commanding officer who is doing his job.

I call the quality having the heart of a captain. Only a few of my contemporaries have it, I think—Mike Lefever, Denis Army, Roy Balaconis, a few others.

Am I among them? Who can say? Time alone will tell.

26 Boardings

They are, in the ultimate sense, the reason we are here, steaming at a stately place, re-creating the gunboat diplomacy off the lonely coast of Haiti of the late nineteenth century.

The prohibitions are simple: guns and fuel. The rationale is to prevent such dangerous things from falling into the hands of the totalitarian rulers who run the country, thus encouraging them to give up and permit the restoration of democracy. Hard to see how this will get the job done. My guess is that it will probably require real combat power ashore at some point.

But, in classic verbiage, mine is not to reason why, but to stop, query, and board suspect merchant vessels heading into Port-au-Prince.

And so we do that.

The boardings are dangerous. I have a group of my people trained in everything from weapons to pressure-point holds, from the layout of merchant ships to small-boat ladder rigging. They are a mixed group, mostly handpicked by me, who are, as we say in the Navy, large and in charge. Big, strong, capable men who are not afraid to be in command of a dangerous situation. They are led by Ens. Dave Dymarck, who in another life was clearly a pirate of some notoriety.

The ships who present as boarding candidates are largely classic "tramp freighters" with mixed crews that hearken back to the small barques of the eighteenth century that plied these waters. There are also erstwhile do-gooders bringing huge barges of stores into starving Haiti. The boarding party wears SWAT-team ensembles—Kevlar bulletproof vests, Secret Service–style "no hands" walkie-talkies, .45 caliber pistols with spare clips, heavy knives, dark-blue unmarked coveralls. Topping off most of these dangerous-looking outfits are the flashy and stylish "Oakley" sunglasses that many in the crew, including me, have adopted for the bright Caribbean sun.

We have done two of the boardings, and each has gone very well. The first was the *Coral One,* a tramp steamer carrying pinto beans and wheat flour; the second a tug, MV *Apache,* towing an enormous barge full of Catholic Relief Society supplies. We were forced to divert both because neither master could fully open up the holds to us. Later, higher authority—I hate that term—came back and told us to let the *Apache* proceed, having verified the contents of the ship with the Catholic Relief Society—and, I think, decided that the negative publicity from stopping three tons of food supplies bound for charity distribution was in fact a bit much. Good move, higher authority.

27

On a slightly overcast Friday morning, we pulled into Guantánamo Bay, Cuba, for our first liberty in over three weeks.

What a beautiful natural harbor. Not especially large, but with a wonderfully wide channel leading up to six good-sized piers.

The small enclave is, of course, completely cut off from Communist Cuba. Castro has even cut off the water, even though the United States has a valid indefinite lease and certainly no plan to give it back. It is a reasonably good-sized place, about forty-five square miles, with rough southwestern-looking terrain, a few small ranges, big sweeping views of the Caribbean, some nice beaches. Castro contends the lease was signed with his overthrown predecessor and wants us gone. I suspect we will never leave such a strategic site, commanding as it does the Windward Passage and all of the central Caribbean.

The base is a tiny Navy version of Club Med. It has outdoor movie lyceums; an excellent and large exchange; cheap, duty-free liquor; beautiful beaches with snorkeling, scuba diving, beach volleyball; softball and soccer fields; a nice gym; many interesting small restaurants and clubs. It is a terrific spot for a two-day visit—much more time would permit a sense of boredom and island fever to creep in. But for a quickie, it is a wonderful port, and the crew thoroughly enjoyed themselves.

As did I.

The first day I played (and won) the ship's racquetball tournament, played a couple of innings on the softball team, and hosted a going-away dinner at the quite nice officer's club for four members of the wardroom who are leaving. We drank too much Red Stripe beer.

The second day I played tennis in the morning, went to a perfect ship's picnic, did some coral reef snorkeling, and took about a dozen wardroom guys out for a dinner of Jamaican "jerk pork" at Palmer's Jerk House. We all hit Baskin-Robbins for ice cream after and bought a half-dozen bottles of "Jerk Sauce," a strange, dark mixture of thyme, vinegar, spices, crushed fruit—it resembles a Worcestershire sauce with a Caribbean twist. Palmer's Jerk House was purely Jamaican style, run by two islanders, and it had outdoor grills and all the Red Stripe Lager and Dragon Stout porter you could want to drink. A nice night—a long and interesting discussion with Charlie Martoglio, the XO, about foreign affairs, with a particular emphasis on the situation in Europe and the Russian situation.

One of the best aspects of being the captain of a ship is the chance to be close with a wardroom of young officers, most of whom are trying to think their way through whether or not they want to stay in the Navy. My pitch about the Navy is always very simple and goes like this:

In addition to the obvious goodness of serving and protecting your country, there are three key practical things that make a career in the Navy a wonderful experience:

- You will never work with better people. The chance to be surrounded by high-quality, motivated shipmates is worth an awful lot of money.
- You will lead a life of high adventure and travel. Where else can you bang around the world on a destroyer, shooting the occasional Tomahawk missile, and, when on liberty, walk ashore in a series of wonderful and historic cities—Hong Kong, Singapore, Sydney, Auckland, Tokyo, Alexandria, Naples, Palermo, Athens, to name a few I hit in my first three years at sea on two different ships.
- When it comes time to leave the Navy, if you have made it a career, you will have an excellent retirement plan that will serve as a safe basis while you go on to other adventures, still a relatively young man or woman.

It's a hell of a good package. And your office at sea will always have a spectacular view. As John Paul Jones said, "Sign on young man, and sail with me."

28

We got the ship very gracefully under way from Guantánamo Bay on Sunday morning, twisted in the wide turquoise channel, and headed fair out to sea. At the moment, we are rocking slowly in a beam sea, just enough to be pleasantly interesting, and I'm thinking about all the early-out requests I'm dealing with.

Let me explain.

The Navy is, of course, trying to "downsize," that is get people out for a variety of reasons, essentially because we need fewer folks and now have more automated systems (gas turbine engines instead of manpower intensive steam plants, for example). We also need money to recapitalize (buy new ships).

So, a handful of crew members have submitted special request chits to take advantage of this, departing before their obligated service is up.

Most would simply like to spend more time ashore with their families. This ship will be under way for about ten of the next twelve months, and that is very, very hard on families. So, when an opportunity presents itself to get out a bit early, there will always be some who want to take it.

Unfortunately for their plans, the Navy early-out program is really targeted at people sitting ashore doing very little—not at frontline Sailors in a great ship about to deploy to the Mediterranean and Arabian Gulf.

So, I must disapprove virtually all of the chits (authority to do so is vested at my level) and spend a great deal of time listening to all the assorted reasons they want to go. OK, I don't mind doing so—it is, after all, the very heart of my job, along with driving the ship. but it steers me into the classic problem of devoting about 50 percent of my time to about 10 percent of the people—and all the wrong people—so often it is the marginal performers who are trying to get out, although there are occasional instances of good people who need to leave the Navy for legitimately unique personal circumstances.

So, today I will be a good captain and get out of my stateroom, away from "the quitters," and out with the 90 percent of my crew who are good and motivated and willing to fulfill the sacrifice they signed up for to come to sea.

They are the center of gravity of this ship. To them I owe my time and energy.

29

I feel better today, having spent much of the past twenty-four hours roaming the ship.

All captains are different. Some can govern effectively from the relative obscurity of an Olympian detachment. I think of a captain more as a servant than as a master, so I must know the needs of the crew. The best way to learn the needs of the crew is from their mouths to my ear, through conversation in the thousands of unlikely quiet (and not so quiet) corners that make up a U.S. Navy warship.

Thus, I am apt to be found in conversation in the forward engine room, the sonobuoy storage locker, or the mess decks rather than sitting at my desk doing paperwork. I am lucky in one way—paperwork is easy for me, especially at the moment with my superb second in command, Charlie Martoglio, who sends only photo-perfect documents to me. Thus, I can give each a quick review and sign with full confidence that we won't get ourselves in trouble.

That frees me up for my walkabouts, which occur two or three times a day, and always involve talking to at least forty or fifty crew members each day. I think I therefore have a good sense of what goes on, good and bad, below my decks.

Helping me are a network of people throughout the ship who I think are good barometers of crew morale and sensibility—the command master chief, Stan Brown, who moved his office to a small space next to the chow line so that he sees literally every crew member two or three times a day; the chief master at arms, the ship's cop, if you will, who ensures good order and discipline as well as the kind of good morale that comes from high standards and pride; the career counselor, who has a steady stream of individuals coming and going through his small office, discussing the pros and cons of a Navy career in this turbulent era; the executive officer, of course, with whom I spend about an hour each day at various times covering the topics that ignite and decompress our small city at sea; and many, many others—from seaman to the ship's barber, they all have a story to tell, a data point to contribute, to the tapestry that is the USS *Barry*.

30 Thanksgiving Day in the Windward Passage

I awoke at 0500, after a dozen calls through the short night. We had been tasked with boarding the *Sant Barbra*, a small (eighteen-hundred ton) freighter sailing from Havana to Port-au-Prince.

I walked onto the bridge just as the sun was rising at 0530, and the quartermaster of the watch—the duty navigator—sang out, "Captain's on the bridge," as he is required to do. That information is carefully logged, so that if there is—God forbid—a grounding or collision, my presence is a matter of formal record.

The small freighter was wallowing in a beam sea, about two thousand yards straight ahead. The seas were deteriorating, and small white caps were cropping up ahead. We were running across the seas, trying to create a lee—a small patch of smooth sea—into which to lower our small rigid inflatable boats (RIBs). By the time the merchant had everything open and ready to inspect, my boarding team was prepared to cross the rough seas to his side.

They went aboard, inspected, and cleared the vessel for entry into Port-au-Prince.

On the return, one of the two RIBs began to ship a great deal of water—a fact we learned when the electrical system of the boat shorted out amid sparks and smoke. The other RIB took it under tow and brought it in, and we discovered that the bilge plug (essentially a plug in the bottom of the boat for draining it) had evidently vibrated itself loose. Since RIBs are effectively unsinkable, there wasn't any truly catastrophic potential danger—but still, it was a very uncomfortable feeling to see one of the ship's two boats limping in under tow.

After we finally got it on board, we settled the ship down and prepared for Thanksgiving Day.

We started with a service on the fantail, attended by about thirty crew members. I spoke about thanking God for this good earth, touched by the sun in the Windward Passage; for our country, strong and free; and, above all, for our families far away.

A young mess specialist sang that great old spiritual, "Amazing Grace," as I watched Haiti slip by on the port quarter. A few seagulls flew over. And the sea rolled on, blue and dark and running strong, the distant whitecaps pointing north toward America. Toward home. Don't I wish.

I spent the rest of the day carving turkeys—one on the mess decks, one in the chiefs' mess, and the last one in the wardroom. The spread prepared by our mess specialists was amazing.

Like Admiral Lord Nelson when he was a ship's captain, I spend a lot of time focusing on food. I do believe that food is the morale center of any ship, whether a Roman galley, a sixth rater of the British nineteenth-century navy, or my brand-new Aegis-class destroyer. Long days at sea can be monotonous, so a crew needs and deserves a break with good food. As the grandson of a restaurant owner (a classic Greek diner in Allentown, Pennsylvania), I've grown up in families that value food and the enjoyment it can bring. So, one of my goals is to give my crew an enjoyable experience every time they set foot in the mess decks. And I think they appreciated the great care and concern that went into the meal—turkey, ham, and chicken—all roasted to perfection, all the trimmings, nonalcoholic cider and beer. Really not bad. And the captain carving!

And that was Thanksgiving Day.

31

It is almost December now. About a month into this cruise that seems to linger on and on like a bad cold. Sometimes I feel like I've been under way for six months—yet time is moving, and by the middle of this week, we will leave the Caribbean and head north for two weeks of exercises off the Virginia coast before finally pulling back into home port on the 16th of December, six weeks after the contingency tasking off Haiti blasted us off to the Windward Passage.

A most interesting article crossed my desk today—from an unlikely source—my command master chief, Stan Brown. He is a piece of work, a superb master chief, very young for the job—only fourteen years in the Navy—although, at forty, he is a couple of years older than I am.

He has seen a lot of life, I think. Had many jobs—a trucker, a lumberjack, a state trooper. He is a physical fitness fanatic, a cycler, runner, and lifter in tremendous physical condition. In terms of his facial features, he resembles George Bush senior. (A "handsome George Bush," as my wife calls him).

He passed me an article written in the mid-1980s called "The Warrior," by a martial arts aficionado and sociologist named George Leonard. A few quotations perhaps sum it up best:

> A warrior is not one who goes to war or kills people, but rather one who exhibits integrity in his actions and control over his life. The warrior's courage is unassailable, but even more important are his will and patience. He lives every moment in full awareness of his own death, and, in light of this awareness, all complaints, regrets and moods of sadness or melancholy are seen as foolish indulgences.

The warrior aims to follow his heart, to choose consciously the items that make up his world, to be exquisitely aware of everything around him, to attain total control, then act with total abandon.

Bushido, the Japanese code of the samurai, is perhaps the highest evocation of the warrior creed. "In Bushido the warrior's life was shaped by his awareness of death." And, finally,

We need passion. We need challenge and risk. We need to be pushed to our limits. And I believe this is just what happens when we accept a warrior's code, when we try to live each moment as a warrior, whether in education, job, marriage, child rearing, or recreation. The truth is that we don't have to go to combat to go to war. Life is fired at us like a bullet, and there is no escaping attempts—drugs, aimless travel, the distractions of the media, empty material pursuits—are sure to fail in the long run, as more and more of us are beginning to learn.

You must concentrate upon and consecrate yourself wholly to each day.

Believing you can be perfect is the fatal imperfection. Believing you're invulnerable is the ultimate vulnerability. Being a warrior doesn't mean winning or even succeeding. But it does mean putting your life on the line. It means risking and failing and risking again, as long as you live.

Not a bad theory of life.

32

A few very rough days at sea, coming out of the Windward Passage, through the Crooked Island Passage, and into the central Atlantic.

A great many in the crew have been very sick indeed.

The ship has been pitching violently, that awful vertical movement that no one—not even those with the most experienced sets of sea legs—can withstand.

I put the crew to bed and we sailed until the weather cleared two days later.

A word or two on seasickness.

Everyone—everyone—has symptoms. They vary from very mild (headache, a feeling of heaviness, sleepiness) to truly violent and awful—vomiting, vertigo, complete incapacity. Most people are somewhere in the middle. And experience can teach you, over time, how to cope. Drugs are better than ever, although they will typically make you sleepy and a bit slow on the uptake.

My own situation is mild, and I've learned over the years how to cope.

But lots in this crew are clearly learning for the first time just how difficult mal de mer can be.

34

We pull into Mayport, Florida, over the weekend. After nearly five weeks in the Caribbean, the cool, crisp weather of North Florida is a refreshing change from the rum-and-coke sticky heat of the Jamaican run.

My parents live nearby, in Atlantic Beach.

I spend the two days relaxing with my folks and dealing with the most difficult decision—by far—of my tenure in command.

It begins with a phone call on Saturday night from my command duty officer, Lt. Cdr. Bob Kapcio. A gifted and bright officer who always seems to have bad luck on his duty days, Bob announces that we have someone in the Duval County jail. Shuddering inwardly, I ask who it is, thinking it will be a young junior enlisted person.

I am shocked to hear it is my chief engineer, one of my key department heads, a Naval Academy graduate and a very senior individual indeed to be spending the night in jail for public intoxication and resisting arrest.

As it turns out, the engineer went drinking with several junior enlisted people (mistake number one), then got into a fight with a bouncer (mistake number two), then resisted arrest violently, ending up in the street with three cops on top slapping cuffs on him and throwing him into their cruiser en route to the county jail (huge mistake number three). All in the captain's hometown (mistake number four).

An ugly story indeed for an otherwise quiet weekend in my hometown.

He is released the next day, and now the decisions begin.

Public drunkenness and fighting with the police—particularly by an officer—are career-terminating offenses. I think many in my position would have cashiered him virtually on the spot. I have a very competent main propulsion assistant—Lt. Brent Hale, a limited duty officer (former enlisted man and rock solid engineer)—and it would be relatively easy to send the engineer packing and keep Brent Hale as acting engineer until the Bureau of Naval Personnel sends me another officer.

So why don't I do that?

First—and most important, because I sense in the chief engineer the heart of a good naval officer. As the captain of a ship, I think we have an obligation—perhaps our most important obligation—to create new leaders, new captains. I think this particular officer could one day be a fine commanding officer, and I'm not ready to destroy his career over a single incident.

Second, I don't want to start my command tour by firing a department head—even with due cause. I have always believed in my own ability to fix virtually anyone, assuming the individual is fundamentally smart enough and motivated enough to do the job. This individual is very motivated—indeed, he is among the most earnest and sincere young officers I have ever met. And he must be smart—an Annapolis graduate and naval architecture major, and a masters degree from the Naval Postgraduate School in mechanical engineering.

Third, I think my engineer is a tough fighter, with a warrior's heart—and that we need people like that in the Navy. He is someone I wouldn't hesitate to go into battle with— hard, energetic, self-motivated, demanding, and with a determination to do well that is unquenchable.

Finally, the engineer is a people person, who has the full support of his department in this troubling situation. Today, both the senior enlisted man in his department and the senior officer stopped by—independently—to strongly urge me to give him a second chance. You cannot buy the support of people like Senior Chief Rick Caceres and Lt. Brent Hale; you must earn it, day in and day out, on the deckplates of a warship. And this young lieutenant—for all his troubles of Saturday night last—has earned their support. And thus he has mine.

I call him in, discuss the whole sad affair, and ask him to restrict himself to the ship for thirty days after arrival. He agrees to do so, and the enlisted men with him will receive roughly comparable treatment at captain's mast.

And so it ends.

35

Under way, eventually, for ten very tough days.

We will be joining our battle group and undergoing our very first series of exercises with the ships and squadrons that will make up our deploying group. They include the nuclear aircraft carrier the *George Washington;* two Aegis-class cruisers, the *Thomas S. Gates* and the *San Jacinto;* and a host of other support ships, amphibious ships, destroyers, and frigates.

This will be a demanding, perhaps sleepless time for me.

The command structure in a Navy carrier battle group is, of course, very hierarchical. There is a two-star admiral in command, with a half-dozen senior captains who are, in effect, his "department heads." There is a full captain in command of both of the cruisers; another captain in command of the nuclear aircraft carrier; another aviator captain in command of the huge airwing that embarks the carrier; a commodore, who is my boss, embarked on the carrier; and another captain who commands the big logistic ship.

As a small-fry commander in command of a lowly destroyer, I need a sign over my desk that says, "Nothing important happens here." Just kidding!

Our job is to support both the captain in command of the cruiser, who directs anti–air warfare, in other words defending the group from air attack, and *also* the commodore, who is in charge of defending from surface ships and submarines. Because the *Barry* has lots of combat capability in all three warfare areas, we tend to be tasked by a variety of people, all of whom want our capability. My job is to prioritize, respond, and sort of pick my way through the competing demands on my ship's time.

Should be interesting!

36

We shot our close-in-weapons system today.

The guns are two relatively small (20-mm projectile) gat-tling guns positioned fore and aft in the ship. They are designed to fire a stream (at about six hundred rounds per minute) of small bullets (made of dense depleted uranium) at incoming missiles. Since we are supposed to easily shoot down most missiles at a range measured in tens of miles, this is really a "last-ditch" system, designed to knock out any "leakers" that penetrate our main battery of eighty-mile standard air-to-surface missiles.

The setup for the practice shoot was tedious. A small Learjet flew overtop the ship at about two thousand feet a half dozen times, towing behind a small sleeve target. When the aircraft passed overhead, we were allowed to shoot at the target.

We tracked, we shot, and countless pieces of the sleeve came tumbling down. Our system ripped it apart and scattered its broken parts across the trackless sea.

An oddly comforting feeling, I suppose.

As I watched the pieces of the target come flashing down through the sky, I looked at the endless horizon behind, the late afternoon sun bleeding down into the choppy mid-Atlantic waters.

Eternity, I thought, for the thousandth time out here. When I look at the sea and sky, I see eternity stretching away the countless miles, rippling out from the surface of the ocean to the sky and out beyond.

It seems an interesting backdrop to a steam of uranium ripping through the sky.

*Captain's Mast: The Least Likable
Part of My Job*

It is the process of judging crew members after they do wrong. Of being a judge. The executive officer is the prosecuting attorney, and the chief master at arms is the chief of police. And tomorrow I will sit as judge on a crew member, something I really don't want to do.

The crew member in question was a drinking companion of the chief engineer on the fateful night in Mayport. Like the chief engineer, he imbibed too much alcohol; like him, he resisted arrest. Yet unlike the engineer, he *also* disobeyed a direct order to return to the ship, given both by an officer and a chief petty officer. Thus, his transgression is larger.

Yet, he is a good crew member, a well-liked family man with tickets on a holiday flight to his home in Puerto Rico. Someone who has given a great deal to the ship—but his violation of naval regulation is enormous by today's standards—drunkenness in public, a violent street altercation with the police, refusing direct orders.

The punishments I can assign are quite enormous:

- I can confine him to the ship for up to forty-five days, with each day consisting of both military duties and extra duties.
- I can fine him up to half his monthly pay for a period of two months—in effect a $1,000 fine.
- I can send him to the brig for up to three days of bread and water.
- And I can reduce him in rank by a full grade.

These are seminal, life-changing punishments. For these cases, the punishment is normally "the max," all-of-the-above levies. An enormous degree of punishment, especially given the return from six weeks at sea and the coming holiday leave period.

Imagine calling your wife, from the ship, after returning from an unexpected eight-week cruise, and telling her that because of one drunken night's revels, you will not be coming home for another month and a half. And that you had been fined a thousand dollars. And that you would receive a demotion at work.

How your life would change, I think.

And imagine the expression on your children's faces when they were told you wouldn't be home for the Christmas holiday. And no New Years. And the trip to Puerto Rico was just canceled as well. And why?

Because Daddy had too much to drink and got in a fight with a policeman.

These are hard decisions, and as I go to bed tonight, I am unsure in my own mind what I intend to do about this second class petty officer.

How will his life change tomorrow?

38

The last twenty-four hours have been the hardest of this young command tour.

It began with twelve hours yesterday—from noon to midnight—around the huge, dangerous aircraft carrier *George Washington*. There is a function that destroyers like mine perform for the carriers, called "plane guard." It is where I drive my relatively tiny nine-thousand-ton ship into a very tight station—about fifteen hundred yards—behind the monstrous one-hundred-thousand-ton carrier. The slightest wrong turn by the carrier, and she will cut my ship in half.

Such a fate is not idle speculation. It has happened twice since the Second World War, most recently when the cruiser *Belknap* was hit and almost sunk by the carrier *Kennedy*. The CO of the *Belknap* was court-martialed and disgraced. Interestingly, the son of that CO served as combat systems officer on my last ship and was a terrific shiphandler—best I've ever seen. I suspect his dad was too; but when the carrier hit, he was down in the wardroom watching a movie. When I read about the incident, years ago as an ensign, I thought, "Well, I might not make the right decision as a CO, the great and perfect shiphandling decision that would have saved the ship; but I will at least be in a position to make it—I'll be on the bridge whenever my ship is in plane guard around a carrier."

So, yesterday I chained myself to the bridge throughout the long afternoon—when there was enough light to see the carrier clearly—and through the still longer night, when it was black and overcast and raining hard and all I could make out—only fifteen hundred yards ahead—was the dim light of the landing pattern lights on the carrier. We turned and sped up and slowed down and played in the shadow of the enormous ship—like a dog playing under an elephant that might at any moment decide to sit down on you and end the game rather abruptly. And we came through all right, . . . I was only really nervous once, when the carrier swung around me and faced straight at me, and I could see its bow light a few thousand yards away, seemingly innocuous except when you think of the enormous tons and tons and tons of massive ship hurtling along behind that single white light.

We cleared from plane guard about midnight. For the next five hours, I tried to sleep but couldn't. Tossing and turning, full of coffee and the danger high, I waited, called over and over again by my watch standers, for the lightless dawn.

At dawn, the seas were higher than I've seen them in the mid-Atlantic this time of year. The reason?

The poetically named "North Wall" effect.

When a cold high pressure center hits the warm air of the Gulf Stream—once in a while this time of year—it creates sudden massive seas. Up to twenty-five feet of tossing and turning green water, vision obscured by blowing foam and scud, fully overcast sky without a discernible horizon—that is the bleak end. We haven't hit that—yet.

But this morning was the worst I've seen in long time.

The ship rode well. This class is designed to be a good "seakeeper," a wonderful maritime expression that means it rides smoothly despite the effects of the sea.

When the message came in predicting the North Wall effect, we had a brief moment of euphoria, hoping we would be ordered into port. No such luck, however. Instead, we were ordered north into a storm haven at sea, an imaginary box on the oceans surface, where we patrol hopefully, awaiting the return of good weather.

And that is where dawn found me, the dawn weak and pallid, bleak and gray. And I, tired, drawn, looking forty-five instead of thirty-eight, a bristly beard and two days without a shower, with five ships within a mile of me, a dozen radios chattering different directions, and a complex shiphandling exercise to complete ahead.

By 1300 it was all over. We had spun the ship through its paces, turning and wheeling and exchanging stations with the other ships in the line, stretching me and the executive officer thin, but finally getting it done.

I crashed, but I was awakened by repeated phone calls, every fifteen minutes or so, and I finally gave up and got up and sat listening to music and trying to get ready for captain's mast.

39

The worst aspect of being captain is captain's mast.

I hate judging others anyway, but in particular I hate the sense of taking a life in my hands as one does at a mast. The two cases before me, a young, debt-ridden fireman (a junior engineer) and the second class yeoman, YN2 V____, are both tough. They are both basically good people who are trying hard.

YN2 was thrown in jail for brawling in Florida; the FN K____ was up to his ears in debt and on the road to being thrown out.

Although many a captain would have given more, I "only" gave V_____ thirty days' restriction to the ship; and I gave the FN a verbal reprimand and informed him I was processing him for an other-than-honorable discharge from the Navy.

As the captain's mast concluded, I walked out, feeling diminished myself. Judgment is the hardest of human tasks, I remember writing in a speech for the secretary of the Navy after Tailhook.

And so here I am, rolling fatly in a beam sea, faintly seasick, tired and gray with the effort of learning my job in such vivid and immediate conditions and "burning in" my own approach and beliefs while trying to keep the crew's morale and spirit up where it needs to be during eight tough weeks at sea.

40

And so we returned from the sea. Our voyage ended, as all good voyages must—except for those undertaken by ships that are sunk—with a return to a port.

The mission in Haiti rolls on after our departure, of course. My sense is that it will be a long-term project indeed. There is so little hope in Haiti, given the economic desolation of the island, that it is difficult to predict anything for endless waves of corrupt politicians, international intervention, inefficient aid programs, coups and countercoups, and crushing poverty. A bleak prediction indeed.

But for the *Barry*, the future looked brighter. The "Haitian vacation" had been a good start with a very green commanding officer at fleet operations. She was no longer that "brand-new" destroyer, but rather had some lines of running rust, a little peeling in her paint here and there, and a whole lot of salt on the decks. Time for a fresh-water wash down and a chance to see our families again from nearly two months under way.

We pulled back into Norfolk after nearly eight weeks at sea—essentially my first eight weeks in command—on a freezing, rainy day and moored alongside an Aegis-class cruiser, the *Vella Gulf*. An acquaintance, Lt. Cdr. Nevin Carr, is the XO of the *Vella Gulf*. He is a sharp officer just a few years behind me, and I suspect he will do very well in this Navy. I know so many exceptional midgrade and junior officers—all of whom could be doing vastly better financially "on the outside" as bankers, lawyers, investment managers, as so many of my Annapolis classmates have chosen to do. Yet, the pull of going to sea and working on a good ship keeps people like Nevin and Charlie Martoglio and so many others sailing on this course. The nation is lucky for it.

Laura, Christina, and Julia were on *Vella Gulf*, waiting for the ship, along with about a hundred other wives and dependents. Nothing can be as sweet as seeing your family after any significant amount of time at sea—even a week can stretch a bit, and a two-month cruise like we'd just undertaken can feel long indeed. The standard six-month Navy deployment is truly an eternity, especially when your children are young and growing up so fast.

We went to Chili's for dinner.

41

Christmas came next, and the New Year, a nice break for the new captain. We went to Atlantic Beach, where my parents lived. And we also visited south to Ormond Beach, near Daytona, where Laura's parents were living.

Both Laura and I were lucky to have come from military families. My father was a career Marine officer, who served in combat in Korea and Vietnam, and later earned a PhD in education. His "second career" was as president of Allegheny

Community College in Pittsburgh, one of the nation's largest two-year institutions. He and my mom, Shirley, loved living "in the beaches" of Jacksonville, Florida, on the northeast coast of the state. Laura's father was a career Navy officer, a P-3 pilot, who likewise earned a PhD and became a dean at Embry-Riddle University in Daytona. The two families met in the early 1960s in Athens, Greece, where both fathers were assigned at the American embassy. The families remained in close touch over the years, and somehow I ended up married to the little blonde girl I first "met" when I was eight years old and she was three.

Both of the dads were wonderful commanding officers, and I learned a fair amount of how to lead Sailors and Marines from watching them and listening to them as I grew up.

So, over that Christmas, we all had a chance to carefully dissect Jim's first couple of months in command, and the reviews in that little supportive circle were—not unexpectedly—quite good. Yet, in my mind, I felt strongly I was living my good friend Kevin Green's prescient prediction about the internal feel of command: "Your first six months will be the most uncomfortable, the last three months will be the most dangerous." I was definitely still in the "uncomfortable" phase, and every time the phone rang with a report from the ship, I held my breath awaiting what I was sure would be some disaster—a fire, flooding, traffic accident, or some other crisis. Yet, the holidays passed pleasantly enough, and soon we were back in Norfolk and ready to undertake the new year in the destroyer *Barry*.

Coming out of the holiday blocks, we were quite suddenly in the midst of preparing for one of the ship's two very toughest inspections, the Combat Systems Assessment/Cruise Missile Certification (CSA/CMTQT).

Throughout January, we worked long and hard days and nights to ready the ship for the CSA/CMTQT.

If we don't pass, I may be relieved of command—it is that demanding, and it is taken that seriously by Navy leaders.

42

It is night, and we are under way almost a hundred miles off the coast of Virginia.

Late January, and there are ice floes in the Chesapeake Bay, smoking mist over the freezing waters, and snow in the air. The ship is wallowing very gently in a quartering sea. The combat systems inspectors are aboard, and we have completed the first of two-and-a-half days of inspections.

There are about twenty inspectors aboard, and their job is to tear into virtually every aspect of my ship's extensive combat system—our radar systems, sonars, missiles, guns, computers, and displays—and determine our readiness for combat operations.

In the business of running a military organization, there really isn't any discernible "bottom line" that lets the system know how well the ship or squadron or division is being run; so we invent a "bottom line" of sorts—inspections.

The psychology of inspections is interesting. There are many requirements, some clear and others more obscure. They are typically drawn from many different publications and articulated by the "inspection team." Thus, it is critical to establish early, clear communications with the various inspection teams so that a sound knowledge of what is expected is developed.

As an example, to prepare for our combat systems inspections, we decided to host a lunch for the leading inspectors, invite them for tours of the ship, and have them down to conduct various seminars and training opportunities. That all went very well, and we included it in our January training efforts.

Finally, on a bitterly cold Wednesday (wind chill -35°, thirty knots of wind blowing), we sailed out of Norfolk and began the underway inspection itself.

As I write this, it is night at the end of the first day.

We have done well on parts of the inspection—less well on others. But I am quietly confident that we will succeed in passing. More on all of this tomorrow.

It is good to be writing again in a journal, back at sea. I know there is much coming up that will challenge me; but I think I will do an acceptable job as captain of this ship. So I hope.

43 Disaster

The second—and most important—day of the inspection has gone very badly. We are supposed to be able to perform a localization of submarine contacts, wherein we start with a large box of ocean and then narrow down the possible location until finally—presto—the submarine is in the crosshairs of the fire control system.

Each of two watch sections—about twenty men in each—is supposed to be able to perform the localization, which then leads to a firing solution.

Today, the first section did very well indeed, completing the localization and generating a valid fire control solution. The second section, unfortunately, did rather poorly.

I think they were nervous, unsure of themselves, and perhaps a bit overtrained. In any event, they refused to pull the trigger at the end of the exercise, and instead simply continued to track the submarine. Despite a great deal of pushing and prodding from me, they never quite made it to the firing point.

When we debriefed the event, all of us felt there was very little chance the second section had passed the evolution. That could—conceivably and, in fact, probably—lead to a failure to certify the team of deployment.

What happens now?

I fall asleep thinking of other employment opportunities.

44

At the start of the inspection, my hyperefficient executive officer, Charlie Martoglio, told me that, in his experience, all inspections are essentially the same, each passing through a similar parabola. There would be moments of extreme euphoria, when we felt we'd hit the ball out of the park, and conversely, moments of deepest despair, when passing the inspection seemed impossible. This would repeat itself throughout the three-day inspection.

He was—as usual—completely correct in his assessment.

We have moved from the mild euphoria of the first day to the complete depression at the end of day two to slight confidence at the moment, here on the third day. The debrief will start in a few hours, and I think we have a shot at passing.

The material side (equipment and its readiness) and the training/administration points may have pulled us through.

I have just heard the commodore (my boss) will be coming for the debrief of the inspection. Not unheard of, but it generally means either a very good score (the commodore wants to pat you on the back) or a disaster (the commodore wants to try to push the inspections to let the ship squeak by). I honestly don't know where we sit.

45

Incredible. We had the highest score of the test of any ship in the past two years. I truly don't think we did that well, but evidently the inspectors did.

It seems the measure the inspectors seek is not perfect performance on each and every evolution, but rather a broad sense that the ship is well organized, can train itself further, has the basics right, can execute solid communications, and is well led at the working level—that is, are the lieutenants and chief petty officers up to the task?

In that sense, evidently, we are considered quite strong.

This is obviously a very real tribute to the teams that Gary Roughead and Charlie Martoglio put together, organized, and trained during the long precommissioning period, and I fire off a message to Gary Roughead—now in the Pacific Command headquarters—to tell him about this.

And a good lesson for me: stay steady through the inspection. Clearly, the current philosophy is that it will be the kind of thing you are never sure about until the results are actually posted.

Our score—a ninety—is literally unheard of, and the adjective grade of "Excellent" is almost as rare.

I am very proud of all my guys. And a little quite astonished we did so well. But mostly I am just relieved.

Now we have the weekend in port before getting under way next week for another month of predeployment training in the Caribbean.

46

We got under way in a fog.

It was drizzling and cold and foggy, with visibility within a few thousand yards of the ship. The pilot lifted us off the pier as easy as "kiss my hand," as was the expression in the nineteenth-century British navy, and we motored away from the pier and headed out to sea.

At times I thought I would have to quite literally feel my way through the fog. But my expert navigation team—headed up by a thirty-two-year-old quartermaster chief petty officer—found the right marks and moved us slowly through the channel and out to the pitching sea.

I'm also lucky navigationally in that the best junior officer on the ship, Lt. (jg) Robb Chadwick, has just taken over as the navigator. Son of a retired rear admiral and an Annapolis graduate, Robb is one of those fine young people who simply inspires confidence with his look, his bearing, and his demeanor. Quiet and self-contained in a professional setting, he is a perfect navigator—calm, confident, and meticulous. He has a fine career ahead in the Navy, and this job will give him a good bounce as he moves forward.

47

And now it is night, a Friday night, at sea.

I am tired and ready for sleep, but we are maneuvering the ship in close to eight other destroyers, cruisers, frigates, and submarines. So far the bridge and combat teams have done well. We mistook one signal early today, but we have since settled down.

We did an ice cream social down on the mess decks. Lots of gooey ice cream, toppings, nuts, whipped cream—the works. I thought it would be good to give folks a little break because my sense is that the crew is dragging a bit at the moment. I attribute it to several things:

- Tired of going to sea, this time for another month, with very little in port time ahead with families;
- A little burned out after the very tough combat systems inspection;
- Coming cruise looking hard—we've just learned we'll deploy a bit earlier than planned this spring, and we'll be doing a challenging part up front going to the June D-day celebration in Portsmouth;
- Rough seas—always a bummer on the first night under way.

48

It has been a demanding week of antisubmarine warfare, that greatest of all artistic feats of war—the hunting, finding, and killing of submarines.

Submarines are like steel sharks—quiet, silent, and deadly. They are designed to hunt and kill. Occasionally, it becomes necessary to find and destroy them—to keep open sea lanes of communication, to sweep an area and make it safe for allied shipping. Destroying a submarine, I think, is the hardest task in naval warfare.

The submarine must be found within the roiling ocean. The nuclear ones travel deep—over a thousand feet—and fast: they are as quick as any ship. Many advantages are theirs—stealth, counterdetection range, speed over most ships, sensors. Yet, surface ships have advantages too. They carry torpedoes, both ship launched and rocket thrown, with ranges out to eight miles. Better yet, they carry aircraft that can harry the submarine for hundreds of miles, much like a coon hound can eventually bring down a convict. And they have reasonably capable sensors for picking out a submarine in the depths—sonars with ranges over a hundred miles passively and twenty-five miles actively.

So, our task—that of my ship and half a dozen others under the command of a senior captain—is to find two submarines and simulate killing them. We spend five days hunting up and down the east coast of the United States, searching, localizing, and attacking. At the end of the week, I think we have done well—my ship's tally is fourteen confirmed attacks, and we have held contact on the submarine consistently.

Yet, the submarines have gotten in their shots as well, and they have launched a fair number at our ships.

In a real war? Who knows? I think our surface force gave roughly as good as we got—which is a tribute to the small force of only two U.S. submarines. Of course, this is antisubmarine warfare against U.S. submariners, the best in the business.

Against third-world submarines and submariners, I am confident we could carry the field with an even greater degree of certainly, assuming our attack included aviation assets and, better yet, our own U.S. submarines. But there is simply no question that submarines are deadly weapons of war and have an asymmetric advantage in ocean combat.

49

A missile shoot: two of our deadly standard surface-to-air missiles against targets—one high, one low. And when I say high, I mean high—seventy thousand feet, twice the altitude of commercial airliners. The low shot was only thirty-five feet above sea level and traveling very fast.

My ship did great on this particular test, scoring two hits with two missiles, and leading the pack of some ten ships on station shooting. I am very proud of my guys, who have worked inordinately hard to get the ship ready for the missile exercise.

When both missiles fire, I see the vapor trails leaving the ship, and I feel a tremendous sense of confidence in the great Aegis system.

But it's worth bearing in mind this is quite "canned" warfare, these missile shoots. Unlike our antisubmarine warfare exercises, which are essentially free play, the missile shoots are highly scripted. We are alerted as to target launch times, bearings, and locations. This is done so we don't waste precious missiles in fruitless launches, and also for range safety, to make sure we don't end up shooting a merchant ship steaming through the area.

Overall, however, I'm fairly confident in the ability of the *Barry* and our other Aegis-class ships to do what's necessary in a dense anti–air warfare environment.

50

Three days in St. Croix. A treat.

The only problem was the anchoring coming in. My ship had *never*—that is right—never anchored. And it showed. We were ragged, but we finally got the anchor set, a process that involves veering (letting go) a great deal of chain and then giving it a good, sharp pull. That causes the flukes of the anchor to dig into the bottom and hold the ship firmly in place.

We pulled into Frederiksted late on a Thursday night after a very successful missile shoot, and everyone just wanted to let the anchor drop and hit the beach. But it just wouldn't hold the bottom, and we spent over an hour dragging and trying to set the anchor. Finally, it caught the bottom, and my Sailors loaded up on the rented liberty boats that carry us back and forth and went not so gently into that good night.

The U.S. Virgin Islands are a treat for my Sailors, with plenty of relatively cheap drinks, decent duty-free shopping, lots of sun, and some nice resorts. I rounded up my wardroom and played some tennis, organized some golf, and generally took it easy.

It was also a nice chance to check in with Laura and see how she, Christina, and Julia were weathering the under way. All going well on the home front. I am ceaselessly amazed at Laura's ability to keep everything on an even keel with me gone so much of the time. She is amazing!

51 *Back to Sea*

Quite literally, as we "backed" out of anchorage and spent a rough but ultimately successful morning firing a torpedo on the range off St. Croix. The only irritant was the incompetence of the range personnel, who just don't seem to care how things are handled. Shooting torpedoes is somewhat of a chore for these *Arleigh Burke*–class ships, as our torpedo tubes are mounted on deck and, as a result, get lots of abuse from the sea. On earlier *Spruance*- and *Ticonderoga*-class ships, the tubes were protected in internal spaces in the ship. Thus, our readiness is also an issue in this particular weapons' suite. Overall, however, our folks were up to the task, and we shot our live round smoothly at the artificial target.

It is quite amazing to watch a steel torpedo literally leap from the deck of a destroyer, like a big shiny shark, and dive into the depths. It starts searing with a minisonar mounted in the nose, and if it is close enough to the submarine, it is a hard weapon to evade.

Our second day out was a day from hell, as the saying goes. Four major gunnery exercises, an impromptu visit by an admiral who is running the entire exercise (bringing the ship to essentially all-stop for two hours), and a—happily—false alarm that initially caused us to start heading to a distress signal some two hundred miles west and conduct a rescue.

I am tired and wondering what the next few days will bring. Should be more of the same—long, hard days; frustrating conversations over the radio, sleepy nights with a thousand phone calls. It feels like a country western song gone very, very bad.

On and on it goes. When the admiral left today, he said, "You look like you are really having fun out here." Hmmmm. Some days more than others.

52

Since the admiral's visit, we've had several good days, most notably on the naval gunfire range.

That is an institution unto itself, a throwback to the most ancient days of ships and Sailors against the land—a ship sailing (or today motoring) along a stretch of coastline, hurling shells at targets ashore.

Today, the range of the guns is prodigious—my ship motored four miles off shore and threw large shells thirteen miles into the Caribbean morning, landing on targets far inland.

I spent the day on the bridge, hoping we would pass. As usual, there is a stiff grading policy, and my experience on other ships has not been especially sanguine. Normally, there are communication problems, gun problems, mechanical and tactical failures.

But on the *Barry*, which at times can feel like "the effortless ship," the team was more than ready, the radios worked, the guns fired hour after hour, and the shells hit their targets.

At the end of the day, we scored a 103.5 out of 106 possible points—a new record for the class (not that many *Arleigh Burke*'s have fired on the range, five perhaps), and among the highest scores ever recorded on the Puerto Rican range.

It is almost eerie how well the people do here, how easy it all seems to be for the *Barry*. So, why am I so riven with doubt about our ability? It was like the combat system assessment, where I truly thought we had failed, only to receive the highest score.

And I think back to the first hour on the naval gunfire range, when I saw, for the first time in over twenty years of going to sea in ships, a perfect rainbow over the bow of the ship.

I can barely describe it. I saw on the port bow the start, and it passed up over the gun mount and splashed into the water on the starboard bow. I called the crew topside so everyone could see it. It was the talk of our little town all day.

Sometimes I truly think this a lucky ship, with a perpetual rainbow over it. Certainly I do on days like today, with a score like that.

53

Now the war has started.

It is a mock war, a Persian Gulf look-alike, with my battle group approaching a hostile country, weapons currently tight, with much saber rattling, confused identification, and provocative acts both ways.

Thus far, no ordnance. But that will soon change, as it always does in war games. Yet, this one reminds me that within six months, I'll be captain off the coast of Serbia, perhaps embroiled in a real war.

Every time I have deployed in my career thus far, there has been action of some kind. The last two cruises have been in the Persian Gulf, including Desert Shield/Desert Storm on a west coast cruiser. Who knows what this one will bring. It could be off the Balkans, where genocide and war rages; or in the Gulf, where I've spent more than my fair share of time; or near the horn of Africa, where instability reigns. Gunboats make good ambassadors, as the saying goes, and our flexibility is extraordinary. The *Barry* can easily move 750 miles or more each day and cover vast chunks of the ocean, sailing from one hot spot to the next.

Chaplain from Destroyer Squadron Two Six aboard today. A nice fellow, young and pleasant, Lt. Dale White. He holds seminars about the meaning of life while we bounce around a thousand miles from all we love and cherish. It seems greatly incongruous at a certain level, curiously moving at another. Tonight's seminar: "The Seven Keys to a Loving Relationship." This to a group of men who will spend 75 percent of their days under way this year. Hmmm. There are times when I think that the real mystery is why anyone stays in the Navy who is married.

54 *The Phones*

I cannot escape them. It seems they ring about every ten to fifteen minutes, giving me some bit of information deemed vital to my performance as commanding officer under way—the ship's course or speed, the barometer's rise or fall, the sprained ankle of a crewman or the healed virus of a ship rider, tasking from the admiral, a crisis on the mess decks—the flow of information seems, and is, endless.

I will not escape the shrill ring of phones until long after I leave this place, I think. It is tiring. It is, I am sure, the highest price of command. There is simply never a moment to relax, a moment when the ring of a phone does not signal some new rumor of war, or slight catastrophe, or lurking fear finally realized.

Tonight it is almost 1900, and I am tired. And yet I think I shall receive a phone call soon that will place me alongside the oiler at some late, harsh hour. And I do not relish that; the long, dark journey past all the ships in the battle group, passing within a mile of the carrier and snuggling up alongside the rocking oiler, the wind high and the seas rolling. Night underway replenishments are hard indeed on a ship, harder on a crew. But the oiler must leave tomorrow for something, and she is carrying our mail and parts and precious fuel. So, I am sure in a few moments, the phone will ring, and I'll walk heavily to the bridge to drive this ship through the dark.

55

And UNREP we did. Our first night UNREP, with the seas bad and the oiler inexperienced—to say nothing of me.

We swung around the large, dark oiler's stern at two miles, with the oiler uncertain of our location because of our low radar cross section, we lined up on her wake and silently glided alongside.

I have always felt there is no rush quite like an approach at night. It is as close as we have in the surface Navy to the night landing on a carrier, I suppose. And while it isn't as fast—say fifteen knots instead of two hundred—it does involve far larger and more ponderous shapes. And the potential for disaster is high at times.

The key to a smooth UNREP is starting to carefully observe the wakes of the two ships from a good distance behind the replenishment ship, ensuring you are well lined up early in the process. There are a whole series of visual and radar clues to tell you if you've placed the ship properly. I like to really let the younger officers do these by themselves, perhaps with the XO watching over them from a distance. But at night, I do tend to edge in a little closer, as it is so easy for them to become disoriented.

I like to come in around 140 feet, then ease a bit closer to send over the lines, then come out and ride around 130 or 140 feet. I remember on my first ship, we always came in at 100 feet, and that feels way too close to me. I am always mindful of Adm. Earnest King's remark that "the sign of a great ship handler is never getting into a situation that requires great ship handling."

Tonight Robb Chadwick was driving, and his eye is good and his control of the engines and rudders very smooth. After watching him for a while on the port bridge wing, I take a cup of boiled-down black coffee—a poor man's espresso—and retire to my chair on the starboard side and let the XO practice watching the conning officer.

My executive officer is new to the ship, but not new to me. Charlie Martoglio moved on to his next assignment, and his relief is Lt. Cdr. Ben Goslin, who served with me on a previous ship. I requested him from the bureau and was lucky enough to have the timing work to get him aboard. Ben is a former high school swim coach (and an all-American swimmer in his youth), who came into the Navy relatively late. A fun-loving New Orleanian, he is a counterintuitively expert gas turbine engineer, which balances my greater comfort with tactics, warfighting, and shiphandling, so I think we'll make a good team. I am also committed to improving his shiphandling, which is not bad, but given his background below decks as an engineer, will need to improve before he heads off to command himself.

56

We finished the UNREP, and as dawn came up the next morning just as we broke away from the oiler, I realized the long, demanding COMPTUEX—a month at sea with lots of exercises—had ended, as all good exercises eventually do. We made out pretty well, and I suppose I'd say that I survived, while my ship thrived. Clearly the challenge in the *Barry* for the captain is staying up with the crew!

Now it's back to Norfolk for some briefings, the challenge of some necessary maintenance, more missile shoots, and the "final exam" before deployment—Joint Task Force Exercise, or JTFEX—looming on the horizon.

57

We survived the deperming crib. A what?

Deperming is the process of demagnitizing a ship so that it won't set off a magnetic mine. Chiefly of interest from the perspective of these pages in that it is a very, very challenging shiphandling process in getting this nine-thousand-ton ship into the floating slip—a dock in the river, if you will—even with three tug boats and the advice of an excellent pilot.

But eventually we were in the slip, the cables run, and the shocks are running through the ship with continuous jolts. I hope this doesn't cause cancer. If it does, we're all in trouble because we stay in the ship throughout the process. The other bad part is simply that the gables are old, dirty, and scratch up the paint on the sides. My first lieutenant, who is responsible for the topside and external paint job, is just beside himself. After two days in the deperming crib, we escaped by slipping all the lines, then gunning out at ten knots backwards. Quite a rush, and we almost creased the edge of the slip . . . but we escaped, as a result of a quick fishtail maneuver with the rudder, and we spun around in the channel and headed free and fair to sea.

After this little adventure, we had a couple of weeks in port. Much of the time was taken up with hosting an Argentine destroyer that had been operating with our battle group during the work ups to cruise. It was *La Argentina*, a Meko-class German-built destroyer/frigate. The captain was Eduardo Aviles, a tall, handsome man who spoke reasonably good English—certainly better than my Spanglish—and who led a good crew. Being around him and his team reminded me how universal certain things are in the profession of the sea. Eduardo's bearing, his manner of speaking, his style were all reminiscent of any other professional navy captain. We struck up a strong friendship, enhanced when his lovely wife, Maria de la Paz, came to visit for a long weekend in the States. Together with Laura, the four of us had some wonderful dinners and lunches together, and promised to stay in touch. Despite the slight language barriers, our experiences and backgrounds were quite similar and cut across time and distance.

I was also happy to have a chance to show off the *Barry* to two famous senators, John McCain and Strom Thurmond. Both wanted to see an Aegis-class destroyer, and Senator McCain, of course, was a Navy hero and former POW. They spent a good day on the ship, and the visit was highlighted by Senator Thurmond's comment that he had "never had better food on a ship." We made shrimp gumbo for him, having learned it was his favorite soup, and sent him back to D.C. with a gallon of it "for later." Both senators liked the ship, and I later received letters from both Rear Adm. Bob Natter, our head of legislative affairs, and Capt. Cutler Dawson, the head of the Senate side of the operations. Since both are mentors (and close personal friends), I felt good about helping the Navy show itself to the legislative branch in style. These visits, which are frequent for the *Barry*, given the newness of the ship, are actually very pleasant for the crew and almost always provide an uplift of morale. Sailors love to show off their ship!

58

At sea again for two weeks of exercises. This time its our very, very final exercise—the one that will give us the right to deploy to the Mediterranean as a certified battle group.

Our part on the *Barry* is actually quite small—we just steam around taking the orders of our various bosses in the battle group. It is a time of testing the rear admiral in command, Al Krekich, and his senior captains who are responsible for protecting the carrier, striking ashore, destroying the enemy's fleet, and other complicated tasks. And what happens over the next two weeks doesn't really affect the *Barry*, unless we manage to do something truly terribly wrong—which I certainly hope we don't. Or, I suppose, manage to do something amazingly good; of which it seems even less of a chance. We'll do our best and hope our bosses all look good!

59

We are three—no, four—days into the fleet exercise.

Thus far, it has been like war itself—long periods of complete boredom interspersed with a few moments of pure hysteria and fog.

The first day, we merely transited down from the Chesapeake Bay entrance to the operating area just off the Carolina coast. There we joined up with the aircraft carrier and dozen or so escorts, supply, and amphibious ships that make up our battle group.

We have been assigned a grid sector to patrol, and thus far all we have done is a single two-hour underway replenishment with the oiler the USS *Kanawa*, a huge AO-177-class military sealift command ship. The CO was an acquaintance from Annapolis, who had left the Navy at the five-year point and become a merchant marine sailor. Now he is the master of the *Kanawa*, perpetually at sea, like Ulysses from the Greek legend, and seemingly happy in his life. We spent much of the evolution catching up on the sound-powered phone line rigged between our ships.

His ship was a decent UNREP companion, slugging heavily through the calm, lifeless seas. We filled with gas, hit the engines, and shot away back to our patrol station.

A mock OSA II patrol boat (there are actual Navy ships out here playing opponents) approached at fifteen knots, tried to provoke an incident, then drifted off to try to get a rise out of more-excitable game—she ended up in the midst of the amphibious ships, darting back and forth among them. But we were not yet in open hostilities, so the challenge at the moment was not to be lured into an untoward incident.

An F-14 aircraft overflew us, no discrete identifiers at all, and we covered (targeted) him with our missiles. Fortunately, I chose not to shoot and he didn't do anything too hostile, so the incident passed right off.

At the moment, we are preparing to receive eighteen pallets, some three hundred rounds of gun ammunition at our after station. We'll move it forward under the great gun forward in preparation for the deployment.

60

The ammo is aboard, some of it bright and shiny, some old and corroded, all of it swung aboard on big pallets run across the churning water between the two ships as we cut through the sea. It is interesting to realize that some of the gun rounds were manufactured before I was born, back in the early 1950s. Old ammo—like old soldiers, I guess—never dies. It just gets slung from ship to ship as the deployment dates come around.

After the ammo load, our next tasking was to pick up one of the heavy amphibious ships and escort it to the shore for a mission of recovering pilots downed inland. We provided shotgun services. The ship was an LPD, a large, heavy gray hull commanded by a senior captain. I tried to stay out of its way, which wasn't easy because our two ships were twisting and turning in the rising seas all morning. The situation wasn't helped by the sudden appearance of a dense fog, which made the LPD vanish from sight, even though it was only a thousand yards away.

When the fog hit, I backed the *Barry* out to about four thousand yards and tried to keep track of the amphib on the radar. A frustrating morning, and I nearly, for the first time in years, lost my temper with one of the ensigns who had the conn. The ensign just didn't keep full situational awareness of the danger inherent in the weather and proximity to a big, badly handled ship. I kept it cool, but I had a better and more experienced conning officer take the conn. Inside, I was seething with the ensign's lack of initiative and competence—and he a Naval Academy graduate to boot.

After a trying four hours close to the shore on top of the amphib, I was stunned to receive a call to proceed to the flagship, the distant carrier *George Washington*, for briefings on a "special mission" for the *Barry*. The seas were rising high by this time, the weather closing in, and I was in no mood to fly to the aircraft carrier CV. But the admiral called and off I went.

I hated to hand the ship over the XO and the wardroom. It was, of course, the first time the *Barry* had ever been under way without me—or without a captain, for that matter, as I'm sure my predecessor never left the ship while it was under way. The barometer had dropped significantly, and I told them to run down the seas, heading for a rendezvous with the oiler. Then I strapped into the small Lamps MK III helicopter—my courtesy ride from the USS *Doyle*—and headed off to the carrier.

As the small helo lifted off and headed into the buffeting wind, I found myself looking at the thunderstorm clouds and thinking, I am looking at something. What is it, I asked myself? A moment's reflection, and I felt the cares of the day and the frustrations of the moment drain out of me, along with anxiety for the meeting ahead. I realized that in the face of those big black clouds, which form and reform endlessly over the uncaring sea, that all of this will pass along in its due course, leaving very little in its wake. As Joseph Conrad, the greatest sea writer of the nineteenth century, said of this sort of sight, it is "the magic monotony of existence between sky and water." In the end, I am looking at eternity.

In twenty-six minutes, the helo touched down gently and smoothly on the massive flagship's stable and placid deck—for the carrier, ten times the size of the *Barry*, responds not at all to the wind or the rising seas.

61

On the carrier, I met very briefly with the rear admiral commanding our battle group. He had just received word he was to have a second star, and seemed happy and a bit distracted, as though something important—more important than talking to a commander—was about to happen. That benign distraction, I thought, was the natural reaction of about 99 percent of all admirals to the presence of anyone junior to them. It was something I consciously tried to avoid in the *Barry,* but in fairness, I was, of course, much closer to the people who worked for me—who numbered only 340—than the admiral, who had ten thousand and more working for him.

He told me to get with the SEALs for the special mission briefing, said we were doing a great job—something he tells everyone—and dismissed me.

I wandered into the flag mess and found the SEALs, a lieutenant commander, a lieutenant, and a lieutenant junior grade. All were right out of the movies—attractive, sandy-haired surfer-looking guys. Their plan was pretty loose and basically consisted of the *Barry* using her stealth qualities to sneak into the beach and bring out a SEAL platoon, which had been doing some kind of special operation ashore.

We discussed communications, water depth, night vision devices, signals, procedures. I briefed them back. They seemed surprised I could remember what they just told me. And in a few moments we were done.

I took my charts and scribbled notes back to the *Barry*—after a quick chat with my immediate boss, the commodore—and was safely back in my own wardroom, on the badly pitching deck, within the hour.

62

The past forty-eight hours have been a whirl of "war."

We have been in continuous contact with the mock enemy for the better part of two full days, with antisubmarine warfare being the focus—along with launching Tomahawk missiles against land-based targets and Standard surface-to-air missiles against enemy aircraft that are more or less constantly inbound on the battle group.

Tonight the weather is bad, dirty and foggy, with a bad pitch and roll and many crew members sick. We missed our first window to leave the battle group and will be leaving as a result at 0200 in the morning, as the wind and the seas pick up against us violently.

But we must collect the SEALs, although we'll have to cross two hundred miles of enemy-infested waters to get in and snag them in their little rubber boats.

The good news is that we'll be coming down on all the battle group circuits, in effect hiding from both the enemy and the nagging call of the battle group circuits.

And so I am tired. Two days of nonstop action have taken it out of me. I drag. The master chief tells me the chiefs are worried about me—about my dragging posture, sighing, shaking my head, my low threshold of frustration. This is the kind of thing a good master chief can impart to a captain. I sense it too, and I'll go to bed earlier tonight to try and compensate.

Ah, but the wind is strong.

63

Today we are motoring slowly and quietly across the bay toward our rendezvous position with the SEALs.

En route, we have seen a single enemy frigate, which we dispatched with two missiles. Otherwise, it has been us alone on the great disk of the gradually clearing ocean, a strong sun, and calming seas as we approach the coast. We've passed a couple of merchants, big ones with large cargoes topside; some Cape Hatteras fishing craft; and a single submarine periscope that turned out—thankfully—to be a friendly submarine.

At dusk, we add lights, rig our stealth gear, and slow to seven knots—positively crawling for us—and try to convince the enemy's coastal defense net that we are who we say we are . . . a Cape Hatteras fishing boat.

64

The SEAL pickup went flawlessly.

As I sat on the bridge wing, watching the sun go down—slowly—at 1900, I really understood the meaning of the special forces motto: We own the night. All I wanted was darkness, when my nine-thousand-ton destroyer would simply melt into quiet blackness, radar systems and sonars silent, and become a small blip on a dully watched coastal radar, lit only by the dim bulbs of a "fishing boat."

Finally, the sun set, and we motored slowly the final twenty-five miles in the dark at only seven knots, wondering if the SEALs would make the rendezvous. They were scheduled for a window from 2200 to 0100, and I suspected we wouldn't see them until well after midnight. Yet we had no sooner slowed to two knots at the rendezvous point then I heard the excited call of the OOD (officer of the deck) for me to come to the bridge.

I saw them first with the low-light night vision devices mounted on the bridge wings—two winking, distant lights, tiny and small on the roiling sea surface, closing the ship.

A silenced motor of some kind, and suddenly they were alongside the ship, zipping under the bow, and I turned sharply to starboard and made a lee from the wind.

They clambered aboard, huge and burly in the dark night, four-day beards, loaded with gear. We fed them a hot meal, tossed their gear in a corner of the helo hangar, turned into the wind, and their helicopter arrived and swept them back to the carrier.

And we were left a hundred miles in enemy waters, our SEAL mission complete. I turned the ship away from land and motored gently into the black night.

65

By the time we rejoined the battle group the next morning, my reserves were exhausted, and the insulation was off my wires. It had been a long three or four days since the rough flight to the carrier, the SEAL planning, the constant contact with enemy forces, the two engagements with mock enemy frigates, the SEAL extraction, and the long run through the night to rejoin the battle group.

But as I walked on the bridge, the seas were calm and the sun was strong and I felt good about all that the *Barry* had done for the previous two weeks.

I totaled it up in my mind—we had shot two enemy frigates in quick-draw missile engagements, sinking both; controlled two aircraft that killed a diesel submarine; successfully engaged five aircraft flying at the battle group; launched twenty-three Tomahawks; and safely extracted the SEALs. It was a good run of luck, with no major errors, no hits on the ship—although the other two destroyers out here were both hit, and one sunk.

On the cost side, I was tired. As tired as I have ever been in the six months of command and feeling it in every reaction. I don't tend to be physically tired, but, like anyone else, I suppose, I am less patient, less capable of slowing down to explain, less willing to tolerate error or sloppiness—and that shows. John Keegan chose the title of his classic on leadership in war, *The Mask of Command*, perfectly. It really is a mask, a projected front of cheerful confidence and good humor and professional competence. I strive for it, occasionally succeed, frequently fail, but always try. The last few days, while successful by and large from that perspective, have been most trying.

As we rejoined, we were sent in to take fuel from the big lumbering oiler the *Kalamazoo*. After swerving all over the formation and getting perfectly lined up, we commenced our approach. All was going smoothly; but at three hundred yards out, we got a sudden call from the battle group commander, changing plans and sending the *Kalamazoo* to another operation. UNREP postponed until evening, or later . . . the fog of war.

66

That night we recovered the attentions of the *Kalamazoo* and conducted a perfect sunset UNREP. The seas were like glass, the temperature in the low 70s, and the sun was setting big and red and beautiful just dead ahead of the two ships.

The helmsman barely needing to correct the rudders, the two wakes smooth and perfect behind us, evenly lined as if with a ruler.

I talked with the other CO on the phone line stretched between the ships, gossiping about ports in the Mediterranean and the "green flash" on the horizon at just the moment of sunset, and about life in and after the Navy. The captain of the *Kalamazoo* is a Navy fighter pilot lined up for command of a carrier after his "deep draft," as the Navy calls the "practice round" of commanding a large logistic or amphibious ship before sending a pilot to the crown jewel of carrier command. Like most of the naval aviators in command of ships, Capt. Eddie Fahey had real dash, a good sense of humor, and enough perspective to overcome the lack of shiphandling experience his first twenty years of flying jets provided. He runs a great oiler, and we're lucky to have him in the battle group.

And then we broke away in darkness, an hour after sunset, rocketing away at thirty-two knots from the oiler, watching it fade into the horizon behind us, the moon rising and small fishing boats bobbing on the semicircle of ocean around.

A perfect UNREP.

And that perfect UNREP was a fitting conclusion to an exhausting but nearly perfect final exercise before deployment.

Now we head back to Norfolk for a month of leave, repair, and final preparations before our six-month forward deployment commences. I think the ship is ready—more than ready. But only time will tell.

67 *Deployment Day*

Today, I did something I have waited my whole life to do. I stood on the bridge of a brand-new destroyer, in command, and said the words captains have said for a thousand years in hundreds of different languages, knowing they were off for long, long sea voyages: "Take in all lines."

In a flash we were under way and slipping out into the strong ebb tide off Pier 25. It will be a long time indeed—six months—until we are back in Norfolk.

Been gone a long time from this journal—in port for thirty days. The month in port is the preoverseas movement (POM), which is the all-too-brief segment of time awarded to each ship before it deploys for six months.

Knowing I'll be away from Laura and my two daughters for half a year has made the month ashore painful. Each day, you are looking toward the separation with dread, like a big, empty patch of sea. We tried to fill the time with cheerful excursions to movies and restaurants and the theme parks in the Norfolk area; but it all has a sense of slow-motion sadness about it. As Laura always says, the best day is the day you leave, because then instead of looking forward to something bad—the departure—you are finally starting to look forward to something wonderful—the return.

The ship has invested a great deal in preparing the families for the separation. We've done everything prudence would dictate, including briefings, completing wills and powers of attorneys, producing a thorough "deployment manual," set in place an ombudsman care line both telephonically and via the Internet for the few folks who have such high-tech capability.

We've talked about car repair, emergency response, hurricane preparedness, and a thousand other things with the wives. But nothing can really prepare a family for the onslaught of separation. As Laura always says, deployments make strong families strong, and it often breaks weak families. Hopefully, we'll not have too much breakage in the good ship *Barry*.

Today, our first day under way, has been relatively calm and slow. We motored out into the western Atlantic and are currently waiting for the carrier to call us into a screen Kilo station, a formation wherein all the smaller ships have sectors to patrol in big boxes hopefully far from the carrier. In the meantime, we are doing deck qualification for a group of reserve helicopter pilots . . . boring, but necessary for someone to do it. Tomorrow, the fun really begins—with plane guard until 0300!

68

Today was consumed with preparations for and actually undertaking plane guard duties.

To safeguard the carrier's pilots, a destroyer, cruiser, or frigate is often called to come into station a mile or so astern of the enormous carrier and follow along in its wake. The idea is that if a pilot crashes upon takeoff or landing, a smaller ship is there ready to pick him up.

A great concept—unless you are the captain of the small ship. You tend to spend a great deal of time worrying about whether the carrier—ten times your size—is going to turn suddenly, not tell you what the new course is, and cut your ship in half. This has happened twice in the post–World War II era, and both times led to inordinate loss of life—on the destroyer or cruiser.

We briefed the detail at 1030 and were called into station around 1330. Sailed in the wake nicely through about 1830.

Then we were relieved, unexpectedly and pleasantly, by the USS *Conolly*—a good deal for us.

Thus, my Saturday night turned into something quite benign. Instead of sitting in my chair on the bridge, anxiously but sleepily watching my OODs try to keep us out of trouble, I was able to spend the time writing a few letters, catching up on paperwork, and reading up on the D-day celebration.

I should mention our first destination in this six-month cruise is to sail to Portsmouth, England, where ships from our battle group will participate in a grand re-creation of the D-day invasion along with representatives from all the World War II navies that were there.

An aside: As I read the D-day books, pamphlets, and magazines we've collected, I wonder how my generation would stand up to a Hitlerian force. Could we bring forth the enormous self-sacrifice, the belief in country and principle, the flint-hearted resolve to fight, to fight to the death? I don't think so. I think that, faced with a Hitlerian force today, Americans would—mistakenly—withdraw within the "safety" of our insular world, and become—at least for a time—isolationists. I say "for a time" because if life teaches you one thing, it is that you must take a stand against evil or it will eventually run you down and consume you.

Dark thoughts for a relatively laid-back Saturday night at sea. I hope there aren't any Nazi scenarios out there.

I think I'll go to bed, reading a few more D-day stories before nodding off.

69

The rest of the transit over was a blur of plane guard, communications exercises, underway replenishments, and antisubmarine warfare practice.

One of the highlights, strangely perhaps, was a Memorial Day at sea.

We held a small service on the fantail of the *Barry*, cruising somewhere in the deep Atlantic, en route to England. I must admit that all the D-day reading has caught my imagination. As I drafted a short speech for my Sailors, I mulled over, for the thousandth time, whether our generation could stand in the face of a long war like World War II—and whether we had the right stuff to prosecute it to a conclusion.

I do many speeches on the ship, of course, from impromptu little sets of remarks on the 1MC announcing system about something the Sailors can come topside and look at off the bow of the ship—to longer set pieces at our monthly award ceremonies, where I try to summarize the schedule and current set of priorities. In essence, captains speak to help their people understand the context of the ship's mission and to motivate Sailors to believe in what we are doing.

Here is the speech I gave on Memorial Day, 1994, rolling along in the first month of a long deployment, to the three hundred Sailors of the USS *Barry*. Certainly not a classic, but perhaps a window into how one captain was thinking on a cool spring day at sea, far from his home and his family:

Remember This

Thanks, Ben [executive officer, Lt. Cdr. Ben Goslin, who introduced me]. And thanks to all of you for attending this service. . . .

Today is Memorial Day. What does it mean to the folks back home? Cookouts, a three-day weekend, a road trip, the pool opens, school is almost out, warmer days. . . .

Those are all the good things; but . . .

I think it means something very different to all of us who wear the uniform today at sea in the destroyer *Barry.*

We are rolling in a beam sea, a thousand miles from shore, sailing on a six-month deployment that will bring us in contact with adventure . . . and danger . . . and perhaps, in the end, bring home to each of us the meaning of service.

So, today barbecues and swimming pools and the joys of summer are far from my mind. . . .

Instead, I think of a long line of American heroes and heroines. . . .

In the Second World War, at the Normandy beaches, I think of the young rangers climbing the cliffs of the Ponte de Hoc, under continuous withering fire from the Germans on the cliffs above, climbing and climbing into direct machine gun fire . . . like climbing into the fire of the sun itself . . . sustaining over 80 percent casualties . . . but reaching the top of the cliff and silencing the guns, so the Normandy landings could succeed.

I think of the Korean War, where my father fought as a young Marine captain. . . .

Where the ice and mud and sludge were everywhere, where the Marines sustained terrible casualties fighting thousands of North Koreans. Outmanned nearly five to one in many battles, when they marched down from a place called the Choisin Reservoir, they carried their dead and wounded with them. . . .

And I think of the war in Vietnam, where my father commanded a Marine battalion and my father-in-law flew as a Navy pilot. . . .

A small country far away, where many young Americans died, in the steaming jungles, on the wide rice paddies, fighting a battle with so little support from home . . . in a land utterly different than anything they had ever known. . . .

And often I think of Desert Storm, where thankfully few Americans fell . . . but where I knew one of them well, a shipmate on my cruiser, the *Antietam,* a young electrician named Daniel Moors Jones, who died responding to a casualty in the engineering plant, in the early days of Desert Shield. . . .

And every year on August 20th, the day he died, I think of his family, reaching out for the flag that was draped across his coffin, wondering why of all the hundreds of thousands of sailors and Soldiers and Airmen and Marines in the Desert War, it was their son who had to die. . . .

I think of *all* of them this Memorial Day, of all the men and women who have died in the service of this great nation.

And I hope you do too . . . for today is their day.

In fact, on this cool spring day in the central Atlantic, I look at the best crew any destroyer captain could ever have.

And I know some of you will stay in the Navy for a long career . . . and others will leave the service and return to civilian life . . . but wherever life takes you, I ask that each of you, for the rest of your lives, whether you still wear the uniform or not, remember *this* Memorial Day in 1994. . . .

On a destroyer called *Barry,* sailing in the deep waters of the mid-Atlantic, a time when you served your country well and truly, wearing the uniform of your nation. . . . I want you to remember this day . . . and on some other day, in the distant future . . . when you reach into the cooler for a cold beer on a Memorial Day yet to come . . . I hope you will pause, just for a minute, and remember *this* ship and *this* crew and *this* cruise . . . and *this* Memorial Day. . . .

And lastly, remember how you found time in a busy, busy day—so long ago now—to walk onto a sunny, rolling deck and honor all those who went before you and paid a high price indeed for the nation we all love so very much.

God bless you, shipmates. . . .

And God bless the *Barry*. . . .

And God bless America.

We have six midshipmen aboard from six different colleges. All seem like impressive young men in different ways, although two of them have told me they have no interest in the surface Navy and instead are interested in the Supply Corps and intelligence, respectively.

I have always been confused as to why on earth you would sign up for the Navy if you want to do anything besides drive ships or submarines? If you want to fly, it might make more sense to join the Air Force, although the challenge of landing on the rolling deck of an aircraft carrier has obvious appeal to the very daring. Yet, I suppose the basic allure of going to sea has an appeal, even for those who aren't directly in the ship line of business, and of course we're lucky to have good pilots, supply officers, and intelligence officers who support what we do at sea so well.

Still, I spend time with all six, coaching them on the bridge, on shiphandling, on leadership, on life at sea.

I feel unbelievably old at thirty-nine talking to midshipmen in their early twenties. They are so utterly unformed.

And I look at my face in the mirror, the faint lines around my eyes, grown from looking into too many dawns at sea after long night watches.

My thinning hair, the hard cheekbones, the thin, frequently tired face.

It is the mask of command staring back at me in the mirror, I suppose.

God, the midshipmen are so young. Too young to be at sea.

We rolled through dense channel fog the night of the 1st of June, with visibility closed to within twenty yards of the ship.

The fog signals boomed their mournful message, and increasingly as the night wore on, I began to sense that we wouldn't be able to enter port on time.

I spoke with the CO of the USS *Doyle*, Cam Ingram, and we agreed that if the visibility was still socked in, we wouldn't enter port but would anchor in man-of-war anchorages until it lifted.

We turned around the Isle of Wight, still in dense fog at 0800, with a 1000 pilot pickup scheduled. I spoke with the crew on the 1MC, telling them we might be delayed entering port.

I hate disappointing the crew, especially on the first port of the cruise. But a strange port, with shallow water, isn't to be taken lightly.

Then at 0900 the fog began to lift, and by 1000, as the pilot boat made its way out to us, the weather cleared to the horizon, and we were able to enter port on time.

All I could think of was the long, long, long line of Royal Navy ships that had preceded me on this course, headed home to Portsmouth, driven by the legendary captains of naval history—the long blue line led by Admiral Lord Horatio Nelson—and that strangely, oddly, and improbably I was now a part of it.

71

The course to Portsmouth Harbor is laid out along a shallow and challenging transit up a narrow channel. Fortunately, we had an excellent pilot—an ex-chief pilot from Gibraltar—who seemed very competent. He had come up from command of tugs, which, I believe, is the best background for a pilot.

He gave us excellent advice without being in the least overbearing, and the transit through the gates to the port turned out to be pleasant and relatively easy.

We spun the ship in the channel and pushed her into berth with a navy band playing away on the pier. We had only twenty-five feet clearance to HMS *Glasgow*, our host ship, astern and about twenty-five feet to a Polish destroyer, also here for the commemoration, ahead. But Dan Carr, my roly-poly first lieutenant and an excellent shiphandler, kept her lined up as the tugs moved us laterally to the pier, and in the end, all was well.

The visit was a treat, with squash matches with HMS *Illustrious*; a wonderful formal dinner hosted by Viscount Cranbourne, the first sea lord; a visit from the defense minister from the House of Lords; wonderful interaction with the COs of a Belgian destroyer and a British frigate; a tour of HMS *Victory*; an excellent pub lunch with the CO of HMS *Glasgow* and his family, our sponsors; and all too quickly the order to sail three days later!

One particularly pleasant part of the experience was interacting with Cdr. Dick Twitchell, the captain in the *Glasgow*. He not only opened up his wardroom for a very warm reception, to include special cocktails and song singing ("You take the high road, I'll take the low road, together we'll meet in Glasgow"), but he also arranged for a superb VIP tour of HMS *Victory* by my wardroom. The *Victory*, of course, was Nelson's flagship and the scene of his death. It was an honor to tour her, and she is very well preserved at Portsmouth. It is possible to stand on the spot he was standing when a bullet struck him down with a fatal shot. The ship is a magnificent reminder of all that navies can do for their nations, and the hospitality of the *Glasgow* and of Dick Twitchell was also wonderfully evocative of the relationship of the Royal Navy and the U.S. Navy.

Here's how we arrived: At dawn on the 5th of June, the flotilla got under way from Portsmouth, led by the *George Washington*, and performed a naval review by Spithead. The idea was to re-create the sailing of the invasion fleet before the actual landings on the 6th of June. So, we anchored the night before, the 5th, after an uneventful crossing, and watched the sun go down over Normandy Beach. It looked, I suppose, like any other beach—except when you began to consider the number of young, promising lives extinguished on those quiet, sandy stretches of beach a half century earlier.

I walked through the decks of my quiet ship all that long night, talking to the young seaman and fireman, in their late teens and early twenties. And I thought of the young men, fifty years earlier, who waited out another long, dark night on the 5th of June 1944, preparing to throw themselves into the furnace of combat the next morning.

All those young lives.

73

The morning of the 6th of June broke gray and overcast, with a smart chop setting down from the northwest. At anchor all around us were U.S. and Allied ships, dozens, all commemorating the anniversary of D-day.

Dominating the vista was the aircraft carrier *George Washington*, moored just outboard of the *Barry*. We were closest to the beach, serving as the immediate backdrop for the president's speech from Coleville cemetery. Around us, farther to sea, were the many other U.S. ships in our battle group: the *Austin, Tortuga, Doyle, Dallas, San Jacinto, Thomas S. Gates,* and many other U.S. ships—and, as well,

Allied frigates and destroyers from France, Belgium, Greece, Poland, and many other Allied countries.

We spent the day watching the various ceremonies on the beaches, about a thousand yards away.

Then at early dusk, at perhaps 1600, we weighed anchor, twisted the ship with engines and rudders away from Omaha Beach, and cut out for the channel, clearing the *Dallas*, a Coast Guard cutter commanded by Jim Hull, a National War College classmate, by a couple of hundred yards to starboard and the massive aircraft carrier by the same distance to port. Tight. We sailed past the cruiser *Normandy* and shaped a course for our next port, in Ireland.

And all along that transit, I kept thinking about D-day fifty years earlier, the huge enterprise capped by so many deaths and the dedication it must all have taken. I hope our military today could measure up the standards of what our fathers did, so many years ago.

74

So Ireland lay ahead, home of John Barry, for whom my *Barry* is named. And you can't be sad on a voyage to Ireland.

The fog hit us again in the middle of the night of the 6th as we wallowed in light winds heading north in the Celtic Sea. At dawn we were—again—fogged in.

But as we came within fifty miles of southern Ireland, the fog lifted and turned into just another gray morning.

By the time we picked up the pilot about two miles south of the Cobh/Cork breakwater, the sun was starting to peek through. The first full beam hit the beautiful cathedral that dominates the village of Cobh (pronounced "'kov") and we safely navigated the narrow, twisting channel leading to the city jetty.

We worked with the pilot to spin the ship and were pushing in close to the pier by 1500, greeted by a crowd of three or four thousand citizens, highlighted by Irish school children who had been given the day off and had gathered to watch the ship arrive.

A wonderful port visit.

We held a reception the first night, with many of the Irish talking of their "connections," as they—there is no other word—guzzled our wine and beer. The Irish are like the Greeks—hearty eaters and drinkers, outgoing, friendly, and they love a party. A great start.

Later we ended up at John Mansworth's pub, the oldest in Cobh, drinking Guinness as smooth as black cream until the small hours.

Dawn the next day was all too early.

75

At 0800 I was up and driving in a long, two-and-a-half-hour sedan ride—across some of the prettiest country in the world—to Wexford, the birthplace of Commo. John Barry.

I was matched up with Charlie, an Irish commander, who spent all the two hours regaling me with Irish stories, jokes, tales, myths, and legends—everything from Yeats to Synge to the Black-and-Tan War.

We laid a wreath at John Barry's grave and then returned.

The night was taken up with dinner at Clifford's, a wonderful *Gourmet* magazine–recommended spot in Cork. I had black blood sausage, a warm grilled salmon salad, and wonderful roast lamb. For dessert, a strawberry shortcakelike dish—all wonderful and for about $50. We had some excellent wine—a French white Bordeaux and a California merlot.

Later that night, we again went pubbing at Mansworths, and I talked politics until 0300 with two Irishmen. A great time.

76

The under way was smooth and professional, and we were off to our next commitment, Operation Swordfish off the coast of Spain.

We were working with about a dozen different ships and submarines from six countries. Close order work, generally five hundred yards or less, with sonars pinging, radar systems flaring, missiles at the ready. They play like cowboys here in the western Mediterranean, and I don't like it.

But we survived three days of craziness with the Italians, Portuguese, Spanish, French, and others, and I've lived to tell the tale.

77

Next stop was Rota.

Spain is white and hot and sunny. The base is flat and calm, and I played tennis and went for two good meals—one at a fish place out the Puerto gate and down past the Plaza de Toros to a small green square at the foot of town, and the other at an Argentinean-style beef house. Both had wonderful cheap ($4) wine—*vino tinto*, which is red wine in Spanish—and terrific food: baby calamari at the seafood place and marinated beef and a warm vegetable salad at the Argentinean place. Got out of both for under $15.

We sailed from Rota late in the evening—about 2200. The sun was setting and the water calm and blood warm as we set a course for Toulon.

Laura will be coming to Toulon a couple of days after we arrive. I can't wait. There is something tremendously romantic about stolen days in the middle of a cruise.

78

Toulon was, for me, the best port of the cruise so far.

First of all, it was really two ports as things turned out. We were initially moored (for three days) at a pier quite distant from Toulon proper. It was a defueling pier situated near a small French fishing village called La Mandrier.

After we tied up the ship, Ben Goslin, my exec, and I jogged up over the pine-covered hill in front of the ship, headed toward the sea. As we came stumbling down the winding road, dodging the Renaults and Citroens, we found a tiny, independent fishing village—the hamlet of La Mandrier.

What a pretty little place. A horseshoe-shaped rade (harbor), with everything from fishing dories to pleasure yachts tied up in the basin. A small beach—with the traditionally topless French women in evidence—and a series of small bistros, bars, petite restaurants, and brasseries.

We passed a pleasant three days there, visiting La Mandrier, the small fishing village each afternoon and evening after the ship's work was done for the day. Had a great dinner up on the side of the island at the house of an American SEAL stationed with the French special forces near La Mandrier. We bumped into him while having Juliper beers at a small brasserie at the crook of the harbor the second night in port. He turned out to be a USNA graduate and friend of our chief engineer. A most interesting young man, well read, athletic (obviously), and living in a gorgeous small French villa with views out over the southern Med.

For dinner, we took home Paella Valencia, prepared in a small shop—it came with the enormous paella, starters of puff pastry with lobster sauce, and salade and garnishes—all for about $20. Wine was available in plenty up at Vic's house. The party included Vince McBeth, the operations officer; Ben; and me. A wonderful evening, and a highlight of Toulon.

I'm so pleased with the ship's operations officer, Vince McBeth. He is an African-American USNA graduate, where he was captain of the football team and an all-American in 1987. He was also a 3.0 plus math major—a smart, focused, and disciplined individual. I met him first in Long Beach, California, where he was on a frigate and came knocking on my door when I was exec in the *Antietam*, an Aegis-class cruiser. Vince asked how he might get into the Aegis program, and I was able to have him assigned as the combat information center (CIC) officer in our cruiser, where he worked for then-Capt. Bob Natter. When I was assigned to the *Barry*, I asked the bureau to see if Vince could come and be the operations officer, and I've been thrilled with his work. He is steady and sure on watch, his people love to be around him, and he clearly has all the intellectual and leadership skills to go a long, long way in the Navy. One of the best parts of this job is helping identify the best young officers around and make a path for them, as others did for me some years ago. I am starting now to think about how we could get Vince lined up for an early command opportunity and hopefully to a good graduate school. Perhaps the Fletcher School of Law and Diplomacy, where the Navy sent me. Why not? Vince would be spectacular.

Other nights in La Mandrier included drinks at Vic's house with a group of his French special forces friends, a restaurant dinner at Mamie's in the port of La Mandrier, and a wonderful luncheon on the French ship hosting us—the *Suffren*. I also played the top tennis player on *Suffren*—a young lieutenant—and beat him easily. Score one for U.S. tennis.

A great three days.

79

The morning we were to move the ship was flat and calm.

I was happy because I'd seen the mistral, the great west wind of southern France, blowing the afternoon before. And I really didn't want to move the *Barry* around a strange harbor, with foreign pilots and oddly handled tug boats, with a fifty-knot mistral bearing down on the ship.

The pilot was the same French commander who had helped us into the pier, and the tug arrangement the same, very European. Two big tugs at the head and stern, with two smaller pusher boats for lateral movement. They use the "push-pull" method, which we do not use in the states, but rather than insist that they do something they are not used to, I can adjust the handling of the *Barry* to their methods.

Lt. Terry Mosher, my weapons officer, drove the ship over and did a wonderful drive. Terry is a gifted and natural shiphandler, probably the best I've got. He has my complete confidence when he's conning, so I spent most of the time on the bridge wing talking to Vince McBeth about coming operations. My bridge team is becoming very smooth, and it knows what I like to see and what my comfort zone is. They are doing a wonderful job, and I'm very proud to see how they have advanced from the very green group I received on turnover last October.

Toulon can be divided into two periods: Before Laura and After Laura.

This is the story of Before Laura.

We tied up at a long pier next to the *Clemenceau*, the large French carrier, and began the repairs to our fuel tank that had brought us to Toulon in the first place. For entertainment, I would leave every day about noon, in the rental car, with four or five officers, and we'd explore Toulon.

We had lunches and dinners all over this intriguing seaport city, which is actually quite blue collar—at least by Riviera standards. Clearly, it is the best buy on the Riviera, with a good French fixed-price dinner going for under $20 for three courses and frequently with wine thrown in!

Pizza in the wood-burning ovens is excellent. My favorite place, in fact, was a pizzeria called Luigis up over a hill behind the beach area of Mourillons. The Cercle Navale (French officers' club) has excellent buys on lunches. The large Carrefour in the downtown is a French Kmart of sorts, with great buys on wine, pottery, and other typically French items.

I scouted the hotel Laura and I would stay in, the Tour Blanche at the top of the city, where the cable cars pass. I saw the room, on the top floor, which included a very complete breakfast—wonderful.

And mostly I just waited for Laura, practiced my French, and went running a few times.

80

On a Friday morning, Fred Pffirrmann and I drove to Cannes.

Fred is my combat systems officer, the third senior officer in the ship after me and Ben Goslin, the exec. He is a fabulous officer, bright, smart, eager to please, and very thorough. His people love working for him, and he and Terry Mosher, who is the weapons officer and his immediate subordinate, make a fine team.

The drive was hot and dusty, over the inland motorway, and we arrived at the Hotel de Ville (city hall) hot and sweating, even in our whites.

The meeting with the Cannes city officials about the coming 4th of July visit was typically French. A great deal of loud conversation, much confusion, good will interrupted by the need to make dramatic points, and ending with much still to be decided.

The legendary Avery Glize-Kane, president of the Navy League of the Riviera, was there, along with her sidekick, the efficient Michelle Fezziola. Both were charming, helpful, and friendly.

After the meeting, they steered us for drinks to the Noga Hilton, where I met the general manager, Richard Duvauchelle, and to a long dinner with Harry Kressman and Jennifer at Vesuvios on the Croisette. I then crashed in a room at the beautiful Martinez Hotel, which had a stunning view of the Croisette.

I was up early the next morning, dropped off at the Nice airport by Fred, and ready to meet Laura. Unfortunately, the flight was delayed by three hours. But that gave me time to stroll through Nice, eat some breakfast, read the French papers, and generally get organized. I also picked up our rental car—a diesel—at which I initially balked. But, like much in France, it surprised me by working well.

At noon, Laura's plane touched down, and in a few minutes I saw her beautiful blonde hair flying as she came down the walkway, looking lovely and happy to be in France.

From then on, it was all wonderful.

81

The best part of the ten days Laura was in France was the first four because we were mostly alone.

Days one and two were in the Hotel Excelsior in St. Raphael, which were special.

We walked that beautiful little city, a cross between the glitz of Cannes and the workmanlike charm of Toulon, and had a great time being by ourselves.

We drove up, up, up into the foggy hills to a strange and special barbecue at Harry Glassman's $10 million house in the Parc E'storel, set at the top of a mountain that must overlook a thousand square miles around the sea and the mountains.

We had cherry beer with the owner of the Hotel Excelsior, Marc Courjon. We met his brother David. Both love the U.S.

Navy and have decorated their bar with countless plaques, pictures, and mementos of all the visits by U.S. naval ships over the years.

We had two great pizza meals at a small pizzeria on a side street.

At the end of two days, we drove back to Toulon and checked into the Tour Blanche, where we had another great two days in that simple city.

In Toulon, we shopped, relaxed, walked. Another great pizza dinner at Luigis, a less-than-inspiring meal at the expensive Hotel Corniche (Rocco Tomenelli's, the U.S. naval attaché, one bad recommendation), a great lunch at the Tour Blance, three perfect breakfasts, shopping at the Carrefour and the French mall . . . and all too suddenly, it was time to go.

82

We sailed, found the replenishment ship, reloaded stores at sea, and anchored at Cannes for the 4th of July.

What a week.

Cannes really is the capital city of the Rich and Famous. All is bathed in champagne, the rich, the super rich, and the wannabes are everywhere, turning and gliding on the Croisette, the see-and-be-seen walkway along the old harbor; bellying up to the overpriced hotel bars; seeking out the tony restaurants in picturesque Mougins just north of Cannes; driving the ridiculous cars.

The mayor, Michel, is a perfect French Clinton. The hair, the size, the charm, perfect. He is currently married to his third wife, a buxom brunette who used to be his secretary.

Avery Glize-Kane had set up a staggering program of events for the ship, and they are worth simply including in this journal as a program—otherwise you wouldn't believe them.

Highlights of Cannes:

- Going to the Beach of the Noga Hilton, staying in a perfect room with a huge bed and the largest bathroom I've ever seen in a hotel.

- Staying at the Noga Hilton and becoming friends with the general manager, Richard Duvauchelle. He is one of the most charismatic men I've ever met, big, handsome, charming, fluent in English, with a delightful family. We had them all out to the ship, and he gave us very special treatment, including his family chairs at the head of the Noga Hilton pier, pier space for my ship's boats to drop off and pick up official visitors and guests, a wonderful room, and a great deal of his limited time. His sons Nicholas (11) and Jean-Edward (6) were charmers, his wife Maggie a delight and oh-so-French, his two older children attractive and pleasant.

- The mayor's lunch at the Villa Domergue in Cannes. Truffles and foie gras as the first course, and it only got better. The heat was intense, but we all took off our coats and ties and opened our choker whites and the wine flowed and the French improved and it was all wonderful!

- Barbecue on the ship for five hundred guests, with beer and wine, sit-down tables, an incredible setting on the 4th of July with country western music playing, the French trying to figure it all out, everyone drinking beer on board—quite a setting.

- The indefatigable energy of Avery Glize-Kane and Michelle Fellizola.

- The "bruncheon" at Faye Howard's. A megawealthy woman with another $10 million house, she put on a champagne brunch of omelets, salads, grilled meats, and wonderful desserts at her stunning pool villa with huge views over the entire Mediterranean.

- Catching up with some of our oldest friends in the Navy,

U.S. naval attaché to France Rocco and Beth Tomenelli. Rocco was the former shooter (director of plan launching) on the *Forrestal* with me, who has spent six years in France and will retire this summer. We played tennis three mornings had a wonderful dinner at the Trois Etages in Mougins and a nice farewell breakfast at a small café on the croissette.

The bummers:
- Being so tired of party and reception and talking endlessly in French. Too much champagne. The beach dinner on the fifth night, where Laura finally burned out and had to be taken home. The heat. The dinner in Monte Carlo—too long a drive, little genuine warmth. The drinks at the Ritz Carleton—too many "bought-their-way-in" Americans. The U.S. air attaché from Paris, an excitable and somewhat dangerous colonel who lost his necktie and exploded on several occasions for odd reasons. A man to avoid.

The verdict:

A once-in-a-lifetime experience. The most interesting port I've ever been to. The triumph of being captain. After all, how bad can it be when you conclude you are finally tired of too much champagne?

83

After Cannes, the rest of the cruise will be an anticlimax, I think to myself as we get under way, Laura safely winging her way home.

We shall see if that statement is a self-fulfilling prophecy or not.

We left Cannes and sailed the ship to the Adriatic without incident, passing through the busy Strait of Messina without being mowed down by the endless streams of kamikaze ferries.

Our mission: NATO operations off Serbia.

Since checking in, we've done a reasonably good job with our tasking, which is embargo operations off the coast of the former Yugoslavia.

The United Nations has a total embargo in place, and we are one of about a dozen ships in a multinational force that stops anything from coming in or going out.

My boss is a British commodore, Alastair Ross, who, like me, is short both of stature and hair. He is wildly energetic, hugely magnetic, and a delight to be around. Our first day on station, he came bounding over on the helo for lunch, briefings, and a tour. I think we made a good first impression.

Our start with our own carrier was less successful. A communication misunderstanding between my Red Crown (air control) and the carrier's aircraft control center (Alfa Romeo) resulted in a late launch of an airplane, a nasty message both ways, and chaffed feelings. Then two days later, the carrier had a bad day in their required check-ins with my Red Crown operators, leading to an unpleasant message and a short and exciting phone call from my admiral to me telling us to help out and get the carrier's check-in rate up.

I must say I was feeling a little down.

Then, as it often does, luck turned and the next few days were far better.

The admiral is coming to lunch and bringing the CO of the carrier and the commander of the air group to let us all make up. I received my fitness report for the first ten months in command in the mail, and it exceeds my every expectation—ranking me first of sixteen commanding officers in the destroyer squadron, and full of wonderful, and of course excessive, praise. My friend, Larry Dirita, once said somewhere that every fitness report is an annual "walk in fantasy land" for a naval officer. Well, I enjoyed mine. I am lucky to be in a ship like the *Barry*, which is the reason for the ranking. And it helps put all that we have accomplished in perspective and overcomes the sting of the few speed bumps we've received.

Then last night we did a 0200 boarding. It was challenging but not overwhelmingly difficult. The only problem was that one of the two RIB boats overheated while the boarding team was aboard the Croatian ferry. But it was a benign environment, the seas were relatively calm, the stars were out, and luck was with us. The other boat ran well, we got the team back in one piece, cleared the Josip for Split, and motored off into the starlit Mediterranean night.

84

The admiral came to visit today.

We have an outstanding officer in charge of our battle group, Rear Adm. Al Krekich, class of '64. A lineman on the Navy football team in the glory years of Staubach and postseason bowl games, he is solidly built, down to earth, funny, smart, and very likeable. He brought with him the commanding officer of the supercarrier *George Washington*, Capt. Fred Sprigg, and the commander of the embarked air group, Capt. Herb Coon.

As I've written a bit earlier in this journal, we had a little controversy a few days ago with the carrier. The gist of it was that we on the *Barry* were charged with ensuring the carrier launched some of their S-3 aircraft on time for an exercise and of keeping count of how many *George Washington* aircraft checked in on time. There were some disagreements about our accounting, probably resulting from differences between what the various radar systems on the two ships were seeing. Naturally, my team thinks our brand-new, high-tech Aegis system is "ground truth," but the folks on the carrier are equally passionate about their systems. I think tempers were somewhat frayed on the carrier, and I spent a couple of anxious nights feeling bad. We could have done it better and, frankly, so could the carrier.

I think today's visit was to "bury the hatchet," and it accomplished—I think—exactly that. From the moment the trio came aboard, they were extremely cordial, polite, and indeed, although they are all vastly senior to me, respectful of our ship and its systems. We toured them through CIC, the bridge, engineering, berthing, and all over the ship. Lunch was very pleasant, and the admiral brought up three topics:

- Tail operations. We have a so-called "tail" on our ship, a mile-long cable that carries an array of sonar equipment designed to listen for submarines. I'm always worried we'll snag it on the bottom, which could lead to millions of dollars of damage. I've expressed that to the admiral, and he backs up our concerns over putting our tail in shallow water later during cruise and will pursue them with the type commander.

- Schedule. The admiral says we should plan on more time with the carrier. Does this mean less Red Crown (the guy in charge of the air picture) and more plane guard? I hope this isn't a punitive move—I don't think it is, or at least I didn't get a sense of that. The up side is, to be around the aircraft carrier means better mail, better logistics, better repair support. Also, there is a good possibility for contingency operations if we strike at Yugoslavia, with the Barry as a search and rescue platform—very exciting!

- Engineering inspection. Every year, ships are required to take a big engineering exam called the Operational Propulsion Plant Examination, abbreviated OPPE. There is some controversy over when we should take it. We want it on the way home, not next fall. The admiral thinks we should take it next fall, probably so we won't be distracted during the cruise preparing for it. He asked me to send him a message with our thoughts on it.

After he left, my friend and fellow captain, Royal Navy commander Ian Montcrief, CO of HMS *Nottingham*, pulled his ship up and we returned the crew members we exchanged earlier in the day. I received his biography for the first time—an interesting career, including a job as OPS in *Britannia* and commissioning navigator in *Nottingham*, the ship he is commanding today. He's an extraordinarily creative officer with lots of energy. Just my "cup of tea," pun intended. I hope we can stay in touch.

Anyway, the most interesting comments were from the admiral about some of the coming possibilities for Adriatic operations. Could be a very interesting summer, with a very real chance of combat. While I don't wish that on anyone, it seems the ongoing genocide in the Balkans will eventually require the release of combat before it's all over.

85

The days in Red Crown passed quickly. After a week, it fell into the typical routine—dawn with coffee and cold toast, morning in the combat information center, a quick lunch, an afternoon on the bridge, a run in the early evening, and settling in for a long, long night of releasing messages, evaluating the day's work, and restructuring our process and approach.

We did lots of boardings, both day and night. We undertook difficult exercises, ranging from air control to mock boardings. In the background, the news in Bosnia-Herzegovina grew worse and worse through July.

The peace treaty put on the table by the so-called "contact group" (the United States, Russia, France, Germany, the UK) was initially accepted by the Croat-Muslim side. Then it essentially was rejected by the Serb side, although not in so many words. Then it was rejected by the Croat-Muslims when it became clear that the Serbs were equivocating. So it moves in the Balkans—a dance of violence, crime, and political recrimination and equivocation that comes, in the end, to mean death for thousands in a war that doesn't make sense. Sadly enough, it's a cycle that has been repeated through virtually all of recorded time in this region, as is abundantly clear in the currently popular book, *Balkan Ghosts*, by Robert Kaplan.

And in the background, the crisis in Rwanda deepens, with refugees dying at the rate of a thousand each day in camps just within the border of Zaire. The pictures fix in the mind—seven-year-old girls carrying their baby brothers, both dying of cholera, with the vacant ten-mile stares of children lost in a green desert littered with the bodies of their parents, with the death of all their tiny thoughts and hopes and prayers.

The summer of '94. Makes you glad to be an American to avoid scenes like that back home, and to think there are at least things this country can do to try to make the world—such a cliché but so true—a better place.

86

We just finished a weekend in Thessaloniki, Greece. We left the Adriatic and sailed here over a couple of days, up through the Aegean, to give the crew a break. The water was beautiful, the seas calm, the sun high and hot.

I sailed these waters thirty years ago, as an eight and nine year old, living in Greece, son of an American Marine Corps officer posted to the U.S. embassy in Greece. And now I am returned, sailing as captain of this great ship of war, wondering always if this is real, if I can do what must be done, if I can bring my crew and ship safely back from this cruise.

But Greece—ah, Greece. Cafés everywhere, bright sun, hot breezes, retsina, souvlaki, roast chicken, kiosks, souvenir shops, the alpha and omega of coffee shops, and, of course, the Greeks themselves—dark hair, strong noses and eyebrows, the intense conversation and gesture, the cigarettes, the warm greetings and conversations. I look at them and see my past.

Thessaloniki is a gorgeous city, built around its harbor. Ancestral seaport for the Macedonian homeland of Phillip II and Alexander the Great, the city is immensely proud of its heritage as the center of the old empire. Thessaloniki is full of museums, beautiful gardens, relics from the Alexandrian era—the bones of Phillip, the shield of Alexander, the crown of Macedonia—all in this seaside city.

A long quay wall, seemingly a thousand cafés, prosperous shops, spreading chestnut trees, the coming and going of coastal freighters—a Greek version of Barcelona. I walked the city with Ben Goslin, my XO, eating at little souvlaki restaurants, small cafés, drinking in the little standup bars. Shopped, went for a jog . . . the weekend passed quickly, and in the morning we'll weigh anchor and head back to Red Crown.

Sadly, I think the crew didn't particularly like Thessaloniki. They found it a little slow. Partly that was an accident of timing—we were in over Saturday and Sunday in holiday July, when a great number of the shops and restaurants are closed. And it was hot. And even though it was cheap—beers under a dollar—from their perspective, it was probably a bit boring.

But for me, it was a bit of my own Greek heritage and a chance to simply get away from the ringing phones for a few days. Paradise.

87

A new schedule announced—a port visit in Corfu, Greece!

Everyone is very excited about this one. It is a very sun-drenched, beach-dominated, bar/restaurant/café/club strip on an island on the western side of Greece.

We'll be going in next to a tender, the *Puget Sound*. Unfortunately, there will be a large-deck amphibious ship there as well, the *Guam*, which will be full of Marines and Sailors—all of whom will have just spent three months off the coast of Somalia and are ready to party. Bad combination with my *Barry* Sailors, and I'm a little worried about it.

Still, that is ten days away—an eternity on a deployment. So, no point in worrying about it yet.

What really is on my mind is the collapse of the peace process in Bosnia. Tensions are rising, the Serbs are attacking the UN forces, and the five-power contact group is about to give up and "punish the Serbs" for their recalcitrance in rejecting the 50/50 split.

What can be done to squeeze the Serbs? Tomahawk missile strikes into Belgrade? Tighten the land borders? Declare a no-fly zone over the entire former Yugoslavia? There are options, but there are very few good ones short of really pounding in there with big-time NATO forces. And I don't think any of the European powers are interested in losing a lot of people over this one.

So, we sit out at sea, enjoying tonight our weekly ice cream social—two flavors of soft ice cream, three hard-packed flavors, a dozen different toppings—waiting, waiting, waiting. It is an uneasy place to be, with an uncertainty about it all. At least we have ice cream.

In such waiting places I have spent so much of my career.

The Persian Gulf, waiting for Saddam, or the Iranians, or the Iraqis. The Mediterranean, waiting for the Libyans. The north Pacific, waiting for the North Koreans. I have grown weary of this waiting, wondering why I am so far away from my beautiful wife and daughters, just to wait a few weeks more.

Tennyson said somewhere, about Ulysses, I think, in a poem I can't quite remember, that "all experience is an arch where through gleams that untraveled world whose margin fades forever when I move." There are times I feel like that—like I'm sailing toward a destination that never quite materializes; like a port that doesn't quite appear where it should. And everything stretching on and on before me, the course laid out on a navigator's table with edges just outside my view.

Ah well. Ulysses I am not.

It is coming time to go home from the sea.

88

Is a ship at sea a monastery? A cloistered, secular, hierarchical society adrift on the oceans of the world?

Indeed, there is a curious kind of spirituality that runs through a ship's company, although most (if not all) of the Sailors wouldn't recognize it as such. If a Trappist monk seeks the sanctuary of the monastery to devote himself to contemplation and work, what is a Sailor devoting himself to at sea?

There is little here but work, work, work. A few minor amusements—not dissimilar to the books and quiet games of a modern monastery—but in the end, life on a ship is about devotion to work, conducted for the common good, with an agreed upon construct of rank, structure, order, and purpose. And good shipmates, if it is a good and lucky ship.

To sail in a modern ship of war is not unlike walking into a desert with a few companions. Everywhere around you is nothing but the sky and the distant horizon. There is little outside input and an endless cycle of work and sleep.

From all of that comes—in some—a contemplation that is not, at the end of the day, unlike the meditations of medieval monks. For others, it is inchoate, unrealized—but it is a rare

Sailor indeed who does not find himself or herself at least once a day standing at the rails of the ship, watching the hopeful gentle rise and swell of the ocean, and staring, staring, staring . . . at what?

At the realization that the sea and the sky roll on forever, unmoved and unmoving for all their motion. It helps keep the day-to-day concerns and frustrations a little bit in perspective, I suspect.

89

The past few days have been exciting indeed.

Two days ago, Bosnia Serbs attacked UN peacekeepers and took back heavy tanks and trucks they had previously surrendered as part of the cease-fire. NATO immediately launched air strikes and the game was on.

The first wave of strikes went in on a perfectly calm, flat, hot afternoon while we were alongside a small merchant conducting a boarding.

I hurried off the bridge, turning the boarding evolution over to my executive officer, and ran down to combat. Putting on my headset, the first thing I saw was an unknown aircraft headed straight at the *Barry*. The circuits were alive with the sound of tension—people asking who the aircraft was, what the threat state consisted of, whether the aircraft had checked in with us.

All I could think of was the *Vincennes* tragedy, when a brand-new Aegis-class cruiser shot down an Iranian commercial aircraft in the summer of 1987 in the Gulf. Steady, steady, steady, I said to myself and then aloud to my team over the circuit in combat.

The only good news was that the contact was flying high—twenty-five thousand feet. But it had no Mode IV IFF, the friend-or-foe identification system that would ensure me it was a blue (or friendly) aircraft. Likewise, it had not performed the mandatory check-in with us in our role as Red Crown, the air control facility for the Adriatic—which virtually all blue aircraft knew to do. Finally, it didn't have a valid Mode II, the code that would give us a sense of its origin.

We raised the threat condition to yellow and tracked the aircraft, calling on every known circuit, including to the NATO AWACS, call sign "Magic," that is always up over the Adriatic and is the Red Crown partner in deconflicting aircraft, monitoring the Deny Flight operation over Bosnia, and generally helping with force air defense.

We waited. The aircraft flew straight over us and turned slightly east. Now it was heading over *Nottingham*, the fine British anti–air warfare destroyer commanded by my friend and frequent lunch partner in the Adriatic, Commander Ian Moncrief. We were reporting to them that we still had no ID on the aircraft. Like us, they were nervous but inclined not to shoot.

Finally, Magic, the NATO AWACS, called and said they had gotten through on International Air Defense, a universally copied radio circuit. It was an EA-6B electronic warfare aircraft, assigned to the strike package, which had launched from the aircraft carrier *George Washington*—which was over five hundred miles away!

We quickly got radio contact, and I called myself. His call was Stinger 05, and I identified myself as Charlie Oscar, or CO, of Red Crown. He quickly answered he was the Stinger CO, or the squadron commander. We agreed he should have checked in and he apologized. I wished him luck in his strike. Fortunately, he informed us about a trailer, a second stinger, coming up from the south.

We reported out to everyone, and the tension noticeably reduced in the CIC.

For the rest of the evening, we tracked the very successful strikes, providing air control and flight following. We were ready to control and protect a search and rescue mission, part of our training and our reason for being in the Adriatic, but fortunately, all of the aircraft made it safely to the target area.

It was a good night, a meaningful one. In the morning, I told the crew that I thought we'd done well in our combat role, and I think it created a good bounce throughout the ship. People are enjoying the cruise from a liberty and training perspective; but, above all, they want to feel they are contributing to something real and meaningful in terms of a mission. Yesterday's combat contributions were a step in that direction.

90

We are anchored in Corfu, Greece.

It is a beautiful, small island just west of the mainland of the Peloponnese. Here Homer thought Odysseus paused in his journeys. Here the ancient Greeks thought Jason and his Argonauts found the Golden Fleece.

We now have a group of four Estonians riding us as part of a military-to-military exchange program. They speak limited English and have been here two days. And now we pull into this Westernized beach-dominated, sun-worshipping island—so far out of their culture they look dazed. Who knows? Perhaps MTV will prepare them for all of this in time. At any rate, they suffered a major disappointment when I was forced to keep them aboard—no visas—they looked *quite* sad.

The rest of the transit down from the pressure of Red Crown and the Adriatic was uneventful, almost peaceful after the hectic pace of the last month. At the start of the cruise, I called Red Crown and the Adriatic "the mountain we must climb" in the middle of cruise. It was, in fact, more demanding and far harder than I thought it would be.

Part of that was my fault. I underestimated the leap from simple single-ship operations to what is essentially battle group–level air management. I should have spent more quality time with my team, training them and focusing them. This is a part of combat tactics I know and understand well personally, having served as both operations officer and executive officer of two separate Aegis-class cruisers, both in combat operation in the Gulf. Yet, we have so much former cruiser experience on board that I assumed (awful word) too much.

But not to make too much of that. We hit a couple of air pockets, speed bumps in the slipstream of cruiser-level operations. All in all, I doubt either of the other two Aegis ships in the battle group did significantly better—although simply by virtue of having a senior captain in command, they would have avoided some of the slings and arrows that came the way of this lowly commander.

All in all, I'm quite pleased and proud of the team. No wonderful messages or kudos, no one else seems to be getting them either, but I have a very real sense of accomplishment and happiness with our job in the troubled waters off the coast of Bosnia.

And, at the end of the day, that truly *is* the essence of command—knowing that the only person you really, deeply, truly have to please . . . is yourself.

At any rate, I'm off to Corfu for some retsina and souvlaki and a little shopping.

91

We are steaming placidly north through the central Mediterranean, bound for the French naval review off the coast of Theoule, France. Tomorrow at dawn, we'll join up with about forty ships, arranged in four columns, and steam within two or three miles of the Riviera, all along its glittering length, from Villefranche, to Toulon.

It feels like I've spent the summer in the south of France, between ten days in Toulon, a week in Cannes over the 4th of July, and now this four-day sojourn in Saint-Raphaël.

Earlier in the cruise, Laura and I spent a weekend in Saint-Raphaël at the Hotel Excelsior, run wonderfully by two brothers, Marc and David Courjon. They are half English and half French and seem quite pleasantly taken with the American Navy. Laura and I had a wonderful time with them, and I'm going to tour them around the ship later this week.

This is one of the nicest aspects of command—pulling into a city where you are taken in, an immediate if quite minor celebrity, simply because you can drive the great gray ship. It is a great experience, and it is magnified on cruise.

It is also important—critically important—to realize how ephemeral it is, how fleeting, how Andy Warholesque these fifteen seconds—not even minutes—of fame really are. Not insincere exactly; because the appreciation is, in fact, based on a real respect, I think, for the job of command, the pressure of the captain's responsibility. But it's not really about YOU—it's about the position you occupy. A good thing to remember in keeping your feet on the ground, Captain.

Anyway, I'll be in Saint-Raphaël tomorrow, on stage again, playing captain.

And after that, we're headed into Naples for a ten-day, midcruise overhaul. It will afford the chance to the crew to see yet another country, another port, and to do a bit of traveling, given the length of time of our stay. Laura and I are planning on her returning for a second visit, which would be lovely.

What I *want*, of course, is to be in Naples, with Laura, who is coming over—the only fame I want in her eyes.

92

Napoli has come and gone.

What a wonderful time—Laura arrived just on schedule and looked, as always, beautiful. We had a romantic time at the lovely Hotel Paradiso high on the hill overlooking Mergillina.

The Mergillina is a district on the southern side of the Bay of Naples, a mile or so from the port, but a universe away from the hustle, bustle, traffic, and smog of Naples proper.

Highlights? The great pizza at Da Pasqualinas and Port D'Alba; the day trip to Capri, with the hike to Tiberius's castle on the northeast edge of the island; the shopping on the back-streets of Naples for espresso makers and cups; the basketball at Carney Park with Vince McBeth and his wife, Elizabeth; swimming, reading, playing a little tennis. But most of all, just spending time with Laura without the press of endless social and protocol commitments like those we faced in Cannes.

The reason for the stay in Naples was simply to do some low-level, basic maintenance that all ships need after three months of hard sea time such as we'd just undergone. So, we pulled into the old port, doing the uncomfortable "Mediterranean moor," where the ship backs in stern first to a slip. A bit scary, but once you're in place, it makes for an easy getaway. The port engineers swarmed all over us, I signed out with a cell phone number, and I went roaring off with Laura for some rest and relaxation.

Before I knew it, it was time to go!

The under way was extraordinarily smooth. We didn't use the tugs or the pilot, although both were available. Simply slipped the lines and heaved around on the anchor. I adjusted the position of the ship on the anchor chain by using the engines and rudder, and we headed up fair and out the channel just after 0900.

We swept through the Strait of Messina at dusk. The visibility was crystal clear—best I've seen in a dozen trips through those normally hazy waters. We found a hole between two ferries and shot through at twenty-seven knots, leaving white water and Italian ferry boats bobbing in our wake. It felt good to be back at sea again.

Incredibly, we have less than three months left in the cruise. The next seventy-five days will pass quickly, I hope, but at a minimum, I'd like to accomplish a variety of personal and professional goals:

- Safely navigate and maneuver the ship
- Meet all operational commitments for MISSILEX (missile exercise) Sharem, Red Crown, and Operations Sharp Guard, Deny Flight, and Provide Promise
- Work out every day
- Eat sensibly and well, losing about five pounds
- Read a dozen books
- Finish and mail *Division Officer's Guide* to the Naval Institute Press
- Produce rough drafts of three TACMEMOs
- Write a letter each day

Somehow, I doubt I'll get through that list, but writing things down is good for the soul and might even lead to getting a few done.

93

We sailed through the central Mediterranean on the smoothest seas I have seen yet this cruise. Clear, light blue, and utterly smooth. You felt that if you stepped from the fantail onto the surface of the ocean, you wouldn't sink but merely be held on the surface, as if on a trampoline.

I've been tired and a little sick—a passing flu, common to many on the ship. I think a bug we must have collectively picked up in Naples is to blame.

A day out of Naples, the barometer dropped and you could, for the first time, feel fall in the air. The temperature was still warm, but the freshening breeze has a hint of coolness in it, like a faint promise that summer is passing and soon, soon, we can go home again.

The schedule for the last seventy-five days of cruise is brutal—seventy-one days at sea, only four in port. We'll be deathly tired of these gray walls by then—as if we weren't already, despite all the pretty ports.

Still, the crew seems to be taking it well and has adjusted to the sentence in jail. After all, Dr. Johnson said a ship is only a prison with a chance of drowning; not a bad description.

Yet we will try to make it less so.

Food should be fairly good. Tim Morgan, our brilliant supply officer, is constantly working the underway replenishment schedules, and he assures me we have lots of charcoal for barbecues, good things stocked up for special events, and the food is always pretty good anyway.

We'll have some special events too—ice cream socials every Friday night, nacho nights with taped football as soon as the games start flowing in, pizza delivery nights, burger and fries delivered, a milkshake night, a chili-making contest, and so forth.

We'll have a miniature golf tournament, crazy hat Fridays, a swim call or two, a video for the home front, fitness program, darts, chess, Trivial Pursuit tournaments, PACE classes—all designed to make the time pass.

Time's arrow is pointed straight at us right now—and we need to hear it whiz by as we turn our heads and look home.

The change of command on the USS *Barry* in October 1993 in Norfolk, Virginia. The commissioning captain, Gary Roughead, is on the left. He has gone on to four stars and is now the chief of naval operations. The author is on the right and is a four-star admiral in command of the Joint Combatant Command in Miami, U.S. Southern Command. If you'd told either of the two that was how the story would turn out, both would have laughed. *(Author photo)*

The USS *Barry* (DDG-52) crashing through the waves. This photo was taken in the fall of 1993, when the ship was brand new. She is an *Arleigh Burke*–class Aegis guided-missile destroyer. *(U.S. Navy photo)*

The author with Deputy Secretary of Defense (and later Secretary of Defense) Bill Perry, second from the right. To the author's immediate left is the fleet commander, Adm. Hank Mauz. They are touring the ship in late 1993. *(U.S. Navy photo)*

Laura Stavridis, at the author's home in Little Neck, Virginia, near Norfolk. Mother of two and author of *Navy Spouse's Guide*. Much of the material in Laura's book was inspired by our tour on the *Barry*. *(Author photo)*

The author with the chief of naval operations, Adm. Mike Boorda, during a visit by him to the *Barry* in early 1995. Before his tragic death several years later, Admiral Boorda was an inspiration to the waterfront, having attained four stars and become CNO after rising through the ranks from seaman recruit. *(Author photo)*

The author on the HMS *Victory* in Portsmouth, England, in spring 1994. The port visit was the opening event of the fiftieth anniversary of D-day. *(Author photo)*

The author and Laura Stavridis together on the island of Capri in the summer of 1994. Laura came over twice during the six-month cruise, once to Italy and once also to the south of France. *(Author photo)*

The *Barry* sailing through "the ditch," also known as the Suez Canal. The ship was en route to the Arabian Gulf with the carrier USS *George Washington* to respond to a threat by Saddam Hussein to invade Kuwait (again) in the late summer of 1994. *(U.S. Navy photo)*

A tired but happy ship's captain in the CO chair on the right side of the bridge wing as the *Barry* heads back through the Suez Canal to the Mediterranean Sea after responding to the crisis in the fall of 1994. *(U.S. Navy photo)*

Conning the ship during a particularly breezy underway replenishment en route to Norfolk in the fall of 1994, after deployment. *(Author photo)*

The *Barry*, being pushed to her berth in high winds in the winter of 1994. *(U.S. Navy photo)*

The Battenberg Cup, awarded annually to the top ship in the Atlantic Fleet. On the left is Lt. Cdr. Mike Franken, the ship's superb executive officer, and the author is on the right. *(Author photo)*

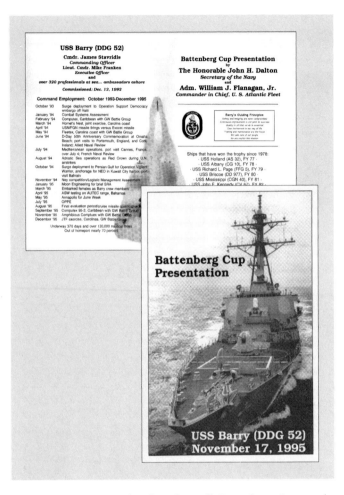

From 1905 to 1940, the three-foot-tall Battenberg Cup trophy (named after Prince Louis of Battenberg) was awarded to the victor of longboat rowing competitions between British and American sailors. Since 1978 it has stood as a symbol of operational excellence within the U.S. Atlantic Fleet, given annually to the ship whose crew has most distinguished itself in battle efficiency competitions, as well as in improvements and achievements in operations, administration, and leadership.

I feel tired this morning. It is the 1st of September, and we are wallowing in a lazy beam sea, drifting on the missile range in the Sea of Crete.

We have been here since early this morning, hoping and waiting for the range to clear so we can get our missile shot off. On the range with us are the USS *Doyle*, a guided-missile frigate (really a lightly armed yacht, some wags would say— although their two helicopters, which we lack, are a huge capability) and the USS *Santa Barbara*, a heavy ammunition oiler with helicopters whose function is to pick up the target drones after they splash into the sea.

I hate missile exercises. Because of the inordinate safety concerns, they have become the very worst of Kabuki theater, scripted to the finest point, overcommunicated, and essentially meaningless.

To some degree we have become a navy that specializes in safety, communicating, inspecting, engineering, administering, retaining, and counseling. There is too little emphasis on shiphandling, warfighting, battle repairing, and leading. I wouldn't want to overstate that, and I know we can hold our own with anybody at sea; but we all need to know that the essence of why navies exist is to fight and win at sea.

As an example of how we are a bit out of whack is that if I charted my personal time, I suspect I spend virtually my entire day working the first list and precious little devoted to the latter. I am actively seeking to reverse this tendency, at least in the *Barry*, but it is a course with some danger.

If I completely reversed my priorities—and focused exclusively on shiphandling and warfighting, I would be in some danger of being relieved for cause within ninety days. This would be because I would fail some major inspection, have a Sailor report my command to his congressman for extreme callousness, or irritate a bureaucrat in my chain of command for failing to report an inventory of hazardous material. Or

I might fire a missile with a commercial airliner within fifty miles (although it would be completely "safe" in a real world sense), or improperly request something for my ship.

Those are the realities. And the good news is that we *are* safe, we do retain good people, we are fairer and more mindful of sensitivities, we are administratively efficient, and lots of other excellent things. The bad news is that our sailing and fighting skills are not what they could be and are withering a bit—some would say badly.

Fortunately, the opposition is even less organized, motivated, and certainly more poorly equipped than we. Not too much terribly bad can happen when the mission is blockading Haiti, Bosnia, or Iraq.

But in some not-too-far-distant decade, I think ships will be hit by cruise missiles, they will sink, men and women will die bad deaths. And hard questions will be asked about the Navy of the 1990s and its priorities and beliefs.

All of this from a morning on the missile range? I *am* tired.

But let me explain the Kabuki theater of it all. The objective is quite simple. A target is flown at the ship, and we shoot a missile at it. A reasonable facsimile of what might happen if a third world country launched a coastal missile at us.

Yet, here are the safety, administration, and communication requirements to conduct this exercise.

An enormous chunk of ocean must be clear and free of merchants, sailors, fishermen, and all manner of boats. They don't pay any attention to the global notices posted or calls on the radio, so that, to begin with, is frequently a hopeful proposition. Numerous communications circuits must be arranged between the launch platform ashore and the ships in the exercise. Countless briefings must be held to verify everything. On my own ship, we brief and rehearse endlessly, hour after hour, all the procedures and drills, running little mock scenarios across countless screens and launching hundreds of electronic missiles like so many games of Nintendo.

Yet, in the not too distant day, the Bosnians will launch against us without warning, without briefings, without safety nets or rehearsals, and without mercy.

Will we be ready?

Perhaps, but with no thanks of this day's missile exercise, during which we now have the fourth delay in four hours for the following reasons:

- A sailboat sails within thirty miles of a possible launch envelope.
- A drone target doesn't launch on time.
- A drone target has a faulty altimeter and falls into the ocean.
- A merchant ship sails within twenty miles of a possible launch envelope.
- Everyone breaks for lunch in the Kabuki theater.

We will re-don our masks and paint after a fine repast and return to playing war. I will work on my attitude.

95

The missile exploded from the forward launcher, driving through the early afternoon haze at four times the speed of sound.

It destroyed the drone twenty miles from the *Barry*, scattering the target into pieces over the surface of the Sea of Crete.

Despite the frustrations of the morning, the missile shot went flawlessly once the target was finally launched—cheers went up in CIC and on the bridge and in the crowd of Sailors watching on the weather decks.

There is nothing as enjoyable as a successful missile shoot.

Unfortunately, our partner in the missile shoot, the USS *Doyle*, did not fare as well. They have a far less capable system and compounded their problems by shooting too early. As a result their missile failed.

We also had command of the *Santa Barbara*, the drone recovery ship, and the *Doyle* itself.

We were OCE—(officer conducting exercise), and it all went well from our perspective. First time maneuvering other ships in close quarters situations—interesting and it went well.

96

After the missile shoot, we set sail for the Adriatic and duty as Red Crown—we've been there, done that—but now we go back. The Bosnians and the Serbs and the Croats and the Muslims are still going at it just as insanely as when we left, just twenty miles inland from our patrol areas.

And we will float and float and float. We'll be at sea for at least fifty days from the time we left Naples until we finally limp into Palermo, Sicily, our next port of call, in late October.

In the meantime, we've got a series of antisubmarine warfare exercises called SHAREM. Additionally, and more important, we have our duties as Red Crown in the Adriatic to contend with.

As things stand now, our duties here are as follows:
- Monitor, track, and deconflict (I love that word) all aircraft flying over this troubled and complicated area
- Conduct embargo operations at United Nations' direction against Serbia and Bosnia, which means boardings, inspections, queries of merchant ships in the area
- Track surface ships moving through the Adriatic sea area
- Control strike and support aircraft operating as part of Operations Deny Flight (no fly zone) and Provide Promise (humanitarian aid)

- Direct maritime patrol aircraft and antisubmarine warfare aircraft supporting Operation Sharp Guard (UN embargo)

In a word, we'll be busy.

Oh, additionally, there is a busy social schedule out here of what is called cross-pollination (XPOL). This means lots of flights and small boat transfers back and forth between the various ships here.

Example. We arrived on 4 September and immediately have the following scheduled:

- 6 September: COs luncheon on HMS *Brave*
- 7 September: COs luncheon/Fast Rope demonstration on the *Barry*
- 8/9 September: Admiral visit for luncheon on the *Barry*
- 10 September: CO HMS *Invincible* visits the *Barry* for lunch and briefing

So it should be busy, and the time should pass fairly quickly. All to the good!

97

We have spent the last week locked in mock combat with a diesel submarine.

A single Italian diesel boat has largely eluded our big, heavy, overtechnology-dominated antisubmarine warfare force. An interesting week. I have learned a great deal about the in-shore knife fighting of shallow water antisubmarine warfare—most of it rather discouraging.

On our side, a $1 billion Aegis-class cruiser, my own $1 billion Aegis-class destroyer, a British antisubmarine warfare frigate, helicopters, maritime patrol aircraft, and a $1 billion nuclear submarine. We've spent the week chasing the tiny

Italian diesel through these shallow waters, and he's done a pretty good job of evading and getting shots off against us.

Why?

In shallow waters, the advantages tend to accrue to the ultraquiet diesel that can run virtually silent on his battery, choosing the moments to snorkel when we are off station or between exercises.

We've caught up with him a couple of times, but he's caught us twice, launching torpedoes at the *Barry* just as we dropped a vertically launched Mark 46 torpedo on him; and firing clean against the HMS *Brave* at close range and getting smoothly away.

On the positive side, he has not gotten near the high-value units we have been tasked with defending, and our towed arrays have worked far better in these shallow waters than I dared hope. Yet, overall, the week's work—an exercise called SHAREM—makes me wonder two things:

- Why doesn't the United States build diesel boats for these kinds of warfighting applications? I do not think our large, expensive nuclear boats are well adapted to the shallow-water scenario, although there is certainly a range of opinion on that issue.

- Have we built a blue-water Navy that is too figuratively muscle-bound to operate cleanly and well in the dirty environment of littoral warfare? Again, it seems to me there are arguments both ways on this question. Our systems, while not designed for the littoral, have lots of capability. We could probably build something from the keel up that would be capable at the things that happen in the littoral, like fighting diesels, taking on other small vessels, flying helicopters, and doing some level of mine clearance.

We still have a long night's free play ahead. And much data to gather. I hope to put out a message with a quick look at the exercise results tomorrow.

98

Spoke with Laura yesterday. Still two months and six days to go. It seems like forever. How on earth did I ever end up as the captain of a ship at sea, thirty-nine years old and missing my wife and two small daughters day after night after day after night? It don't answer, as the character Jack Aubrey often says in the superb Patrick O'Brian series of novels. It just don't answer.

99

Since finishing up SHAREM, the antisubmarine warfare exercise that consumed a great deal of command time and energy, we have been floating. Floating.

Doing very little. Waiting for something to happen, waiting for a boarding, waiting for a little romance.

In a circle, we steam, slow and steady.

The country appears to be about to invade Haiti, which may bring us home late, well past the 180-day mark.

The administration seems to have not a single idea about what to do to sort out the Haitian problem. Yet, it seems, in all my distant naiveté, so very simple. The only national interest we have engaged in Haiti is not to have boat people. If we merely tow them back in after they set sail, they will soon stop coming. If we show them it doesn't work, they won't come. A "tow back" policy. It seems like a sensible policy, so long as it is applied across the board to all illegal migrants interdicted at sea by the hard-working (and overworked) U.S. Coast Guard. Such a policy should be equally applied to anyone else who wants to come here by sea—or by land, for that matter.

Naturally, there are legal approaches to emigrating to the States that start by *not* getting on an inner tube, and include filling out applications at the U.S. embassy and then either succeeding or, sadly for the individual but that is the way of the world, failing in the petition.

It is also hard to see the justification in losing the life of a single American Sailor or Marine to restore Aristide to power. His administration, even from this great distance, appears quite corrupt.

And I think the Haitians are being underestimated—badly—insofar as their ability as a troubling, sniping, skulking, man-killing opponent. They look quite capable to me of using asymmetric warfare to bog us down badly. After all, we have history in Haiti, not all of it good.

An invasion of Haiti would be the flip side of Desert Storm, which looked hard but turned out easy. I think invading Haiti looks easy but would turn out hard.

However, no one is asking my views. Which is how it normally works.

100

A dangerous underway replenishment today.

UNREP is normally fairly routine at this point, but this one was anything but—it was with a British oiler, the *Orangeleaf*, which has a very strange lineup (the arrangement on the deck of the ship sending over fuel, ammunition, or stores).

Today we were pulling alongside the *Orangeleaf*, planning on a routine fuel transfer to our after, starboard station. But as we pulled alongside the larger ship, it became apparent that the lineup would put our bow way out in front of the oiler. The problem with that is the heavy bow wave that pushes back from the front of the oiler, acting on our stern.

The stern pushed out, the bow came in, and I found myself edging in toward the oiler, clipping past the 150-foot point, the 120-foot point, and just inside the 100-foot point— dangerous territory, because within 100 feet, large, wide-bodied ships (like theirs and mine) tend to merge together—a localized Venturi effect takes over.

We managed—just—to keep outside eighty feet and got control of the ship.

All in all, a rough ride and one I didn't enjoy.

The real pressure of command is not to be found in the sleepless nights, constantly interrupted with phone calls; or the need to say no to so many requests; or the passing of bad news on late return from an already long deployment; or the constant, staring eyes that follow and follow you all the day long.

The real pressure of command is, quite simply, that you put your ship's reputation on the line, directly and completely, so very often, and in a matter of what is really motor skills pitted against environmental factors—every time you handle the ship in difficult situations.

"You are only as good as your last sea detail." A great quote, and one that wraps up the pressure of commanding a ship. There are no second chances in shiphandling. When the wind or the current or the fog takes you, and you bounce the ship off the bottom or the buoy or the pier—then you are finished, once and forever, and so is your ship's reputation for a long time.

As I tell the young officers, you can only do the best you can do in handling the ship. And sometimes you make a mistake, like you can do in every endeavor; but in this profession, there are virtually no second chances, no margins for mistake, no recovery of respect.

You and your ship's reputation is shredded and your time in the Navy is finished. Like my friend and classmate, a brilliant fellow and a fine leader, who bounced his Hawaii-based oiler off the bottom, or another friend and classmate, one of the best athletes in our class, whose frigate collided with a replenishment ship during an UNREP. Excellent officers, great mariners; but the single mistake was the final mistake, and it closed out their careers. Worse, their ships suffered a loss of reputation that would follow them for a long time.

So the second piece of advice is equally simple as the first: Don't over invest your whole life in your career. If you do that, you can start to think that if your career goes down, your life goes with it. In the case of the two fellows I just mentioned, both have left the Navy and are doing exceptionally well in the civilian world, as have countless others under similar circumstances before them.

And in a business like ours, where you truly are only as good as your last sea detail, you have to safeguard your life and keep it separate from your career. You have to do the best you can and "avoid situations calling for excellent shiphandling." This day and every day.

101

Been a while since I've written.

It has been extraordinarily busy over the past three weeks, as we have wrapped up our second month as Red Crown. I spent a good deal of time traveling in helicopters between the *Barry* and other ships of the formation: to the *Invincible*, a British carrier; the *Toronto*, a brand-new Canadian frigate; a pair of British destroyers, the *Brilliant* and *Nottingham*; and a Dutch ship, the *Jan Van Brakel*. The meetings were for conferences, discussions, and frequently lunch. Beer was frequently involved—on all except the *Barry*, sadly.

In all cases, I was touched by the friendliness of the foreign navies and by the respect accorded to the U.S. Navy. It was also a pleasure to be able to drink on a ship at sea. On U.S. ships, it is forbidden; we are "dry." They are consistently impressed with the power of our ships and the ability of the United States to forward deploy force. They are constantly amused by our intolerance for drink at sea.

Perhaps the most interesting of the ships was the *Invincible*, an older British carrier. It carries a very small air wing of half a dozen vertical-flight Harriers and about eight Sea King helicopters for airborne early-warning and antisubmarine warfare. While only eighteen thousand tons (as compared to a hundred thousand for a U.S. large-deck carrier), the ships are very capable in the littoral environment. The *Invincible* is in the Adriatic to provide support to the British troops ashore involved in UN operations in Bosnia. It seems to me that our large amphibious ships could easily fill the role of littoral "carrier," with the right load of vertical flight aircraft. Yet another *Proceedings* article I must write one day.

The Dutch ship was coed—about one-third women. Unlike the U.S. Navy, the Dutch navy evidently does nothing to defeminize the women assigned. They have long, styled hair and makeup, and they are heavily perfumed. The ships seem very well run—excellent damage control and topside preservation. I was interested in how it worked because I am starting to hear through the rumor mill that the *Barry* will be the first destroyer in the Navy to "cross the gender barrier." I hope we get the call because I think we could do a good job integrating women into the ship. I've never had a problem with the idea, and I bet the first group of women coming to a destroyer would be highly motivated and capable.

For each visit to a foreign ship, I had to fly in a British or Dutch helicopter. In a word, terrifying. They simply jump in and take off. No checklists, no preflight, no warm-up. They love to scare the passengers with spinning vertical takeoffs, dives, flying sideways. Not too enjoyable, especially as I'm not the most ambitious flyer around.

The only flight I remember really enjoying was a return from the *Invincible*, when I could look through the open door at the sun scoring the surface of the ocean with thousands of tiny diamonds. As the helo flew low over the surface of the sea, the diamonds kept moving and moving, just ahead of the helo, like a wave of light illuminating the path back to the *Barry*.

102

We left Sharp Guard and the Adriatic a few days ago, leaving behind the dangerous NATO oilers, the chatter on the circuits in bad English, the confusing signals, the offshore danger from the Serbs—and landed in the middle of Dynamic Guard, a NATO exercise about twice as confusing and only half as well organized!

Dynamic Guard involves about twenty ships from seven countries—the United States, Turkey, Greece, Italy, Canada, the UK, and the Netherlands. It is spread over the entire eastern half of the Mediterranean Sea, beginning at the southern approaches to the Adriatic and gradually expanding east into the Aegean. It will end up with ten days of amphibious operations just off the coast of western Turkey.

The most amazing historical irony I could imagine is unfolding.

Seventy years ago, in the early 1920s, my grandfather, a short, stocky Greek schoolteacher named Dimitrious Stavridis, was expelled from Turkey as part of "ethnic cleansing" (read pogrom) directed against Greeks living in the remains of the Ottoman Empire. He barely escaped with his life in a small boat crossing the Aegean Sea to Athens and thence on to Ellis Island. His brother was not so lucky and was killed by the Turks as part of the violence directed at the Greek minority.

Now, nearly a century later, his grandson, who speaks barely a few words of Greek, returns in command of a billion-dollar destroyer to the very city—Smyrna, now called Izmir—from which he sailed in a refugee craft all those years ago.

You ask yourself, what happened in those seventy years, from 1922 to 1994? Simple. The United States of America happened.

It is a story that seems to meld together refugees of Haiti, South Vietnam, and Cuba as well as the ethnic cleansing of the Balkans; with the American dream of overcoming and striving and achieving success.

They are all ideas and images that flicker through my mind as I drive my destroyer through a rolling sea, on my way to the land my grandfather was forced from nearly a century ago. . . .

103

Dynamic Guard ended in the oddest way.

The world, as it has twice before for me, exploded in change as a result of a crisis on the dangerous border between Kuwait and Iraq. Saddam moved three divisions of guards troops to the border a day ago, and the world reacted as it has learned to do to Saddam—forcefully and with real power.

Within hours of his movements to the border, the carrier *George Washington*, the Aegis-class cruiser *San Jacinto*, and the destroyer *Barry* were rocketing toward the Suez Canal, bound for the Red Sea.

We broke off from the exercise after a gun shoot, a series of air events, and many controversial confrontations between the Greeks and the Turks. We had a Marine Corps major, Chad Nelson, on board to sort all that out. A good Marine, an A-6 NFO, he kept us all laughing.

When we got the word to break off the exercise and steam at best speed for the Suez Canal, I thought he would cry, he wanted to come along so badly.

But we dropped him off via a 0100 helo ride to the Aegis cruiser in company with us and turned the ship south, heading fast into whatever lay ahead south of Suez.

104

The transit to the Suez was uneventful, and we anchored just north of Port Said at dusk on a Sunday night to await pilotage and permission to go through the "ditch."

I was summoned over to the carrier *George Washington*, anchored a mile away, and met there with the admiral, his staff, and the CO of the *San Jacinto*.

The plan was laid out. The three of us would weigh anchor around midnight and motor through the Suez on our way to the Red Sea. There we would drop off the *San Jacinto*, and the carrier and the *Barry* would proceed around the Arabian Peninsula and into the heart of darkness, the show, the Persian Gulf.

Rear Admiral Krekich, after explaining the plan, asked me how fast the *Barry* could go. I said, "As fast as you need me to, sir." He said, "No, seriously, what's the top end? The carrier can do high speed, but I know the *Barry* would shake apart going that fast." I looked him in the eye and said, "I think we can manage that, sir. If we start to have problems, I'll let you know." He looked doubtful but agreed to give us a try at the top end of the carrier's speed range, which I think we can honestly manage. The only real concern is fuel—the carrier is nuclear powered, and we'll have to take drinks from her every day or so if we are really turning and burning. That means not only a high-speed run, but also constant high-speed UNREPS. Not much sleep ahead for me, I thought, as I motored back to the *Barry*.

I laid down and tried to grab a few fitful hours of sleep, which wouldn't come.

I thought about Laura and Julia and Christina, about the transit, the refuelings, the risk of combat, whether Saddam would make yet another phenomenal miscalculation and plunge the world into war, or whether this would all die in a few days.

I thought about whether or not I liked my job. I wonder what all this is about—blasting through the uncaring sea at high-speed to drive through a sandy canal and bring missiles to bear on a distant country.

I worried about the canal transit, the sharp dark corners of the "ditch," the less-than-perfect Arab pilots, the hot sun on my crew all day, the oily salesmen and harbor masters looking for cigarette bribes, the twenty-four hours on the bridge, watching the tepid water of the canal flow by and by and by.

And I never fell asleep, and I got up at midnight, feeling tired and old, old, old.

105

When I walked onto the bridge at midnight, the moon was bright, and a slight breeze was blowing off the Egyptian shore. It was perhaps 80 degrees, but dark and with a dry warmth.

I talked briefly with my rock-solid officer of the deck, Fred Pffirrmann, and the conning officer, a brilliant young lieutenant, Terry Mosher. Terry had been sea and anchor detail officer of the deck in his last ship, a cruiser, and had motored through the Suez Canal a couple of times. Fred Pffirrmann was the combat systems officer and never missed a trick. Seeing the two of them on the bridge was a reassuring sight.

Around 0100, the carrier weighed anchor, and her massive bulk gradually moved toward the lighted channel of buoys leading into Port Said and on toward the south. She was followed at a respectful distance by the cruiser *San Jacinto*, and then by us.

A mile or so outside the channel, a pilot boarded.

A former Egyptian naval officer, he smoked incessantly, demanded cigarettes and ball caps, and seemed to know very little about his business. I politely gave him a place to sit and focused on the navigation picture with a great deal of personal interest.

We used our radar systems and moved slowly in the wake of the *San Jacinto* and *George Washington* into the channel, gradually increasing speed to ten knots.

After we passed through Port Said, a new pilot came aboard who spoke better English and smoked American cigarettes. He had some dignity and didn't ask for much, only the right to sit in a chair through the long night.

Impressions of the long night watch:

- The pilot stopping at a tight juncture in the canal, dropping to a prayer rug, and praying
- Terry Mosher, walking the ship slowly around the corners in the buoy lines
- The dark, dark lines of the canal and the desert beyond
- The hawk-faced, mustached pilot smoking and brooding and occasionally praying again

"Captain, you can go below and get some rest. I have been the captain of a submarine in the Egyptian navy. You can go below and rest," said the pilot.

"Thank you, I shall sit in my bridge wing chair for a time," I replied. I think a captain leaving the bridge during a canal transit would probably be relieved for cause if discovered by higher authority. And rightly so.

The dawn, gorgeous and cool. Soon turning hot, and the morning baking and baking the Sailors on the forecastle.

Breakfast of blueberry pancakes, hot, without syrup, eaten on the bridge with a pot of strong black coffee.

And the canal winding by, thoughtless of the blood and the treasure spilt in its construction, protection, and conquest over the centuries it has existed in one form or another.

Around midmorning, another pilot embarked, this one younger, not prayerful, actually quite talkative.

"Maouf, R.," said his identity badge. He spoke passable English and wanted "several cartons of cigarettes." I don't smoke and feel strongly about not giving cigarettes as a gift, even to smokers, so I gave him instead a ball cap and a lighter and a signed picture. He seemed put off by my refusal to give him cigarettes.

We anchored in the Great Bitter Lake, about two thirds of the way down, and I downed a quick lunch of fruit—plums, apples, and grapes—and came back to the bridge.

While we were anchoring, there was a disagreement between my navigation team and the pilot. We finally resolved it, but it called to mind the entire issue of confidence, and I was again glad of my solid young navigator, Robb Chadwick, son of an admiral and a fine, fine officer. And my new quartermaster chief, Sam Lovette, a wiry Floridian who grew up on boats and is stubborn and certain with a compass and a divider. They were right and the pilot was wrong—dead wrong. If I'd taken his advice, I could have stopped writing this journal by now, as I would have grounded the ship in the canal. We finally sorted it all out and dropped the hook in the Great Bitter Lake.

The final third of the canal was tiring.

It was seriously hot by this time in the mid to late afternoon, and everyone was tired. Fred and Terry were going strong, as was Rob—but we were all feeling the effects of twenty-four hours straight and the tension of sea detail and all the pressure.

We embarked the last of four pilots at Port Suez, at the southern end of the canal. He was brusque, professional, and the most efficient chain smoker I've ever seen—in and out, lighted and done, and another lit fresh and on the way to his mouth, all in one smooth motion.

He was fat and sweaty and could handle the ship well. He had only a small task and steered us briskly and efficiently into the open sea. We dropped him off, and I felt relieved and free for the first time in twenty-four hours. It had been a long, long day.

106

Since bursting through the canal, we have been rocketing at thirty knots down the Red Sea and will pass Yemen on our way to the Gulf shortly.

We took fuel and stores from the carrier. A smooth operation.

The *George Washington* is a wonderful ship, huge and powerful and friendly in a big, St. Bernard-like way. I wouldn't want to make her mad, but a good ship to have around in a crisis.

It had been years since I'd been alongside a carrier—since the *Valley Forge*? And I was nervous. But as it turned out, it was a glass-calm day, and we smoothly rolled into station and took on the fuel easily and gently, with compliments all around.

Rear Admiral Krekich came down to the carrier's deck to watch our approach and smiled and gave us a big thumbs up as we settled in to take fuel. He's a good leader and makes me feel confident.

107

We have been blasting along at high speed for two days straight, and it will be time to refuel again from the *George Washington* tomorrow. I hope it goes as smoothly as the last.

This is a job of highs and lows.

Yesterday, I was tired from the Suez transit, the pressure of the carrier UNREP, the uncertainty of the crisis . . . and I felt all the weight of command sitting on my shoulders like a brick.

But today, as my beautiful destroyer cut through the water hard and fast at high speed, and the sea spray covered the decks, I walked forward and pushed against the wind and felt like a part of an inestimably long line of captains at sea going into war.

It is hard to describe, the feeling of being a captain sailing into danger.

One part is responsibility for a great ship of war, the feeling that comes from looking at something beautiful and powerful and knowing that you own it truly and absolutely. Another part is anticipation of standing up, of being—yes, I'll say it—a leader in combat. We have so few chances to do that in this postmodern time. But the sea captains are combat leaders, not well known, but known at least to their Sailors. And in the these past few days I have caught traces of it, in the way the Sailors stand a little back and look in a friendly, supporting, trusting way. Their look seems to say, "You can do it, Captain, we know you are good and steady and will carry us all in the end into whatever lies ahead." Maybe I'm imagining it, but it feels good.

And another part of it is pure exhilaration, the joy of battle to come, be it the launching of Tomahawk missiles, or the defense of the carrier with missiles or guns, or the search for Iraqi mines, or any other mission that is yet over the horizon in the Persian Gulf. And the last part is the sense of fear, the uncertainty that means the future holds good, and bad, and indifferent outcomes and that you must step so very carefully to find your way to what is right for your ship, and yourself, and—above all—your crew.

So I walked along the windy deck, on a sunny day, in the southern reaches of the Red Sea, and felt oh so good about my ship, my ship, my ship.

108

On CNN the crisis seems to stutter and stagger. Will it amount to much? The media want it to. The Clinton administration, I think, has developed a very low tolerance for Saddam and his antics. The United Nations as well. Some in the Pentagon must have made the calculation that we might as well load up and take Saddam now, rather than waiting three or four years, for the inevitable lifting of sanctions, the equally inevitable rebuilding of Saddam's forces, and the even more inevitable reattack on Kuwait, all of which will come if we do nothing. Saddam is immutable, a calculating machine that operates with a terribly imperfect vision of the world. The ultimate "garbage in, garbage out" decision maker, obviously surrounded by sycophants and fools who fear to tell him the truth.

And he keeps dragging me to the Gulf.

In 1987, when I was freshly commissioned and deploying the *Valley Forge* as operations officer, Saddam's Exocet missile found the *Stark* in the middle of a dark Persian Gulf night, and there I was, blasting through the Indian Ocean on my way to the Gulf to spend all summer and fall escorting Kuwaiti tankers in and out of minefields, under the barely restrained Iranian missiles in the Strait of Hormuz.

In 1990, as exec in the *Antietam*, I was executing a schedule through the western Pacific when Saddam invaded Kuwait. I spent the rest of the summer, fall, and winter waiting for the war, with a pregnant wife at home, living in anger day by day, waiting, waiting until the release of Desert Storm set us all free. We should have finished with him then.

Now in 1994, as captain in the *Barry*, I am just completing a successful deployment, with nothing left but three nice ports to go and a homecoming, when he precipitates yet another crisis. Geeez. Let's get this over with already. In the Suez Canal, as I was motoring slowly south through the heat and the sun and the dust, the Egyptian pilot asked me what I thought of Saddam. And I said, this time, this time, we will be finished with Saddam once and for all. I hope I'm right, because if I'm not, I know there will only be more pain ahead.

109

On the home front, Laura is as she always is—calm, happy, beautiful, a perfect wife, lover, mother, and person. How I ever became so lucky I will never know. She is the steadiest person I've ever met.

But I call her every couple of days to reassure the network of wives through her, and she is always relaxed and supportive, full of ideas and optimism.

I can't wait to be home to talk all this over with her and relax in front of a fire and just be not on a ship, not in command, not being called every eleven minutes.

The phone just rang.

110

Just completed another underway replenishment from the carrier *George Washington*. That is just getting to be pure work.

Carriers are not supposed to do much underway replenishing, which as I've mentioned, is the operation wherein a small ship nuzzles up alongside and takes fuel while both ships move their massive bulks through the water 100 feet apart at twenty miles an hour—sort of like passing gasoline between two cars moving up the freeway about ten feet apart.

It is a demanding evolution any time, even alongside an oiler that knows what it is doing and how to do it.

Alongside a carrier—which does it perhaps three or four times a year—it is a real white-knuckles ride.

And my knuckles were white yesterday, after two and a half hours alongside, three different conning officers, two helmsman—and only one captain.

We kept yawing in and out, moving from 100 to 160 feet. Hard to say exactly why because the seas were very calm. Yet, the carrier seemed to have a difficult time steering a steady course. I think the seas were deceptively calm, in that there was a very long, gentle, but powerful swell that made the carrier sweep her head on and off, on and off.

They also had a terrible time setting their rig up properly and passing it over.

What should have been an hour alongside turned into two and a half, and at the end, I was exhausted.

All this on the Navy's birthday.

We enter the Persian Gulf tomorrow. Saddam is still on the border. Like 1990 all over again. It is time to put this guy away once and for all.

III

We have been in the Gulf for three days. The first twenty-four hours was very hard. We pounded along at thirty knots, moving northward on an all-night run through the Strait of Hormuz. We were barely a mile—a very close distance in a dark sea at thirty knots—from a hundred-thousand-ton supercarrier—throughout the transit.

After sprinting through the strait, we chased the carrier up to the north Arabian Sea, a 100-mile run, into the carrier operating area. We were challenged by Iranians, Omanis, UAE—everyone but Iraqis.

Within hours of pulling into the Gulf, we were trying to settle out alongside a small resupply ship, the USNS *Mars*. Had a hard time finding the niche. The *Mars* looked very wide at night, and I brought the ship in too wide—about 200 feet, when we should have been in at 150 or so. It made it hard to get the rigs over, and the *Mars* was chiding us over the circuits. But by that time, I was exhausted, my team was exhausted, we were all so tired—after the eighteen-hour transit through the Suez Canal, the five days of pounding along at high speed past the Red Sea and North Arabian Gulf, the all night transit through the Strait of Hormuz—and I just didn't want to take any chances.

So, we moved in slow, got the rigs over, and pulled nearly

forty big pallets (about half-ton lots) of supplies—everything from Xerox paper to tomatoes. We finished about 0100.

Then we crashed, and I awoke at 0500 and went alongside the *Pecos*, a big, comfortable oiler. The carrier was on the other side, so we needed to look smooth—and, amazingly, we did. Everyone was truly running on empty by this time, but we slid into station smoothly, immediately brought over the rigs, and pumped up 260,000 gallons of fuel.

After the UNREP, we moved a few miles away from the carrier, and everyone in the *Barry* slept the sleep of the virtuous. We'd been at sea fifty days, stormed over fifteen thousand nautical miles in ten days, and were very tired indeed.

112

The good news of the past two days is that we have been stationed close to the carrier providing "shotgun" protection—keeping her enormous bulk safe from errant cruise missiles, patrol boats, and all the myriad of dangers that can fill the Gulf. Being close means access to POTS (Plain Old Telephone System), which permits access to Norfolk to make routine calls. So, I've been able to talk to our ombudsmen, Patty Bonner and Susan Hicks, helping them keep the home front relatively quiet, calm, and hopefully largely unconcerned. I've also been able to talk to my boss back at the destroyer squadron to ensure we are on track with all our inspections and requirements. And I've been able, best of all, to talk to Laura. This is all official business of course—no social chitchat—but at least I hear her voice and know that she and the girls are OK.

We talk about the emergency leave cases—the highlight of which is our impossibly young looking (and actually young, just twenty-one years old) Ens. George Olson, whose equally young wife, Ginny, has appendicitis and has miscarried about four months into her pregnancy. Diane Goslin, the far-more-experienced wife of XO Ben, is seemingly constantly ill with a miscarriage herself, an ulcer, kidney stones, a hernia—many problems. The wives as a group, of course, are nervous about our return date, which is increasingly up in the air.

Have I really talked about why we are here?

On the 4th of October, Saddam Hussein began moving large numbers of elite Republican Guards units toward the Kuwaiti border. Perhaps he thought the United States, tied up with Haiti, Cuba, Bosnia, and Somalia, wouldn't respond to a small move into Kuwait.

As usual, he was wrong.

After our arrival in the Gulf, he evidently rethought his position, and over the past few days, he has been pulling troops busily back toward their initial positions.

The Russians have been involved diplomatically and seem to have brokered an agreement with Saddam that he will (1) move back off the border and (2) recognize Kuwaiti borders. Then the UN will lift the sanctions currently in force against Saddam and Iraq that are absolutely crippling the Iraqi economy.

Not the right move from where I'm sitting. The sanctions are the best thing we have going to keep the pressure on Saddam. Lift them and he undoubtedly will pursue weapons of mass destruction and continue to abuse his people and threaten his neighbors—not just Kuwait, but the far more important Saudi Arabia.

The real threat in the Gulf, in my mind, is not Iraq. It is Iran. With a far larger population, more money, an eye toward nuclear weapons and advanced maritime forces, and, above all, a true revolutionary fervor, the Iranians are the real potential megapower of the region. And although their population is young and perhaps could be brought around to a positive view of the United States, the mullahs and their allies in the conservative movement still hate us for our support of the shah while he was in power.

In my view, we need a democratic and reasonably capable Iraq as a bulwark against Iranian expansion and fundamentalism. In fact, absent Saddam, Iraq could very well be a U.S. ally in the region—as crazy as that might sound today when a hundred thousand soldiers, hundreds of aircraft, and dozens of ships are pouring into the region to threaten Iraq and essentially re-create Desert Storm.

113

The crisis is dying.

Over the past two days, the reporters are leaving Kuwait and our ships in droves, the interest is dying down, Saddam is pushing back rapidly from the border, and everyone is calming down.

The bad news is twofold. First of all, after all this work and a deconstructed schedule and loss of three great final ports, it appears we will not have a chance to shoot Tomahawks, and second, we may—no, *probably will*—get home late. All without a good reason.

On the other hand, we can say—I think safely—that the sudden arrival of very real naval combat power on his shores caused Saddam to blink and pull back. And in the long throw of a career, or a life, it was worthwhile to be a part of what happened here. I am communicating all of this to my crew.

And who knows, there may be twists and turns that we haven't seen here yet. As I am increasingly fond of saying, only time will tell. Hopefully, if we are released from the Gulf in time to make some semblance of our homecoming date, which is just before Thanksgiving, we'll be happy. I think worst case is in early December, and thus we'll miss Thanksgiving and some well-deserved time off. But at least we'll have been part of a challenging response, and we'll all feel good about our part in that.

It is all a part of the price you pay for the right to serve.

114

A lot has happened over the past few days.

We've been anchored in Kuwait City, where we escorted a group of amphibious ships tasked with evacuating Americans from Kuwait in case of an invasion by Saddam.

A long sea detail through minefields cleared in the Gulf war. My team was up all night, and by the time we dropped the hook at 0700 about two miles off Kuwait City, we were all exhausted. The water was a light coral green, and the sea was filled with kelp drifting languidly by in large snowflake-like clusters.

It was a strange feeling to be back in these waters. During the Gulf War, I'd been south in the Central Arabian Gulf, never this far north. This had been Indian country in those days, no place for an Aegis-class cruiser. Our job had been controlling the air picture and shooting Tomahawk missiles, and the in-close work was handled by the frigates.

As I told the crew, by arriving at Kuwait City, we were truly at the far end of the bus line. They could send us no further on this cruise. We were as far from Norfolk, Virginia, as we could go and still be in the area of operations—nine thousand nautical miles, roughly.

From this point, from this anchorage, from this dry and gusty Arab city, every mile we motored was a mile closer to home. That's a nice feeling.

After accomplishing our mission and pulling a small group of U.S. citizens out, we weighed anchor at 1600 on a hot fall afternoon, with a harsh wind blowing off the desert, and detached from the amphibious group, heading south toward a very full day of underway replenishment in company with the carrier. I had the feeling we'd very soon be headed home.

115

At 0500, the 1MC loudspeaker system started to blare. Within a moment or two (or three), I was in the pilot house, watching the first of two underway replenishment ships slip under my stern—the *Mars*. We moved around here and there, and within a few minutes we were taking pallets of stores, both from her helicopters and across the wires alongside. After two hours of tough shiphandling alongside, we broke away and headed off . . . for another UNREP!

The second "event" was an 1100 alongside the *Walter Diehl*, a *Kaiser*-class MSC oiler. The master was the quietest, uncommunicative man I've spoken with on the bridge-to-bridge in many years at sea.

Anyway, we survived. I took a nap and woke up to make a USNA video—after all, for whatever it's worth, I'm Jim Stavridis, class of '76, captain of the USS *Barry*, forward deployed in the Persian Gulf. And from all of us, Go Navy, Beat Army! The idea of the video was to show it at the Army-Navy game in a couple of weeks. Vince McBeth, class of 1987 and the football captain, and Jim Stavridis, class of 1976 and a varsity squash and tennis player—a big guy and a little guy—were in front of about a half-dozen other Annapolis graduates, including Terry Mosher, Rob Chadwick, and others. A fun interlude. I doubt it'll ever see the light of day, but it was fun to make. Vince and I wore our letter sweaters.

Then it was time to brief the navigation detail for getting into Bahrain.

We finished that, and I was settling into my cabin for paperwork when I heard, "Commanding officer, your presence is requested on the mess decks."

I walked down with the supply officer and into the mess decks and the entire crew was there! With cake and ice cream! Truly a surprise. And I knew it was a year in command for me, and I was happy and gave a quick speech and shook hands with all of them before going up and working until midnight. How quickly it has all gone.

116

The next day we pulled into Bahrain for a wonderful three-day port visit.

We anchored out in Sitrah anchorage, exactly where I'd anchored half a dozen times as the exec in the *Antietam*. It was (again) hot and dry, with a strong westerly shamal, the desert wind blowing harshly.

The three days were notable for the shopping (two wonderful rugs, a beautiful gold necklace and bracelet, perfume, brass) and for the sleep. I actually slept through the night each night for three days. So relaxing. All the stress symptoms I've been building up—some well-disguised but internally felt irritability, numbness in my left arm at times, tiredness—all seemed to melt away with a few beers, a good night's sleep, and a little recreation.

Boy, I can't wait to go home.

117

We slipped the anchor on the 25th and motored out into the central Arabian Gulf. We shot through the Strait of Hormuz and into the North Arabian Sea, streaming at the heels of the carrier at twenty-seven knots.

Since then it has been a fairly relaxing transit, with us locked up in escort, simply watching the stern of the carrier churning away a couple of miles ahead of us—still looking big, but thankfully headed away.

The only tough thing was the underway replenishment from the carrier today. We will transit the Suez Canal north late next week, blast on across the Mediterranean at top speed, then make it home—on time—on the 17th of November, just before Thanksgiving.

The mood in the ship is terrific as the schedule firms up.

118   *New Wrinkles*

We will have to take fuel again from the carrier, a difficult evolution on the best days, and as the barometer drops and the weather turns worse (sea state 4 today, with white caps and thirty-knot winds), the prospect is far less than appealing.

Additionally, instead of puttering through in the carrier's wake on the 4th, we'll now be shot through "early" on the 3rd—on our own—and sent racing across the Mediterranean to some "yet to be determined" fueling point. Rota? Gibraltar? An oiler?

The admiral's staff, whipsawed by changing dates, can't seem to pull a plan together. And my ship is snapped back and forth continuously. An hour ago, I had the admiral on the mess decks telling my guys we'd be transiting on the 4th with the carrier—now we go on the 3rd. A sudden dawn refueling. Changes, changes. At the moment, we are blasting back and forth in the Red Sea, turning aviation fuel into noise as the carrier flies meaningless flights.

Boy, I'm tired of this.

It's really time to go home.

119

What a good day to have behind me.

We arrived in the southern anchorage of the Suez Canal, Port Suez, yesterday morning after our fourth refueling from the carrier. The refueling went very well—best we've done to date, in fact. And then we were detached to proceed to anchorage. We slid into V2, the deep-water slot well south of the busy port, and let the authorities know we'd transit the following morning.

Around 0330 this morning, they began to call and try to push us to get under way and lead the convoy through. This would have entailed a tense dark transit through Port Suez, which has the distinction of being the site of more peacetime groundings of U.S. naval warships than anywhere else in the world.

I told them my intentions were to get under way at first light and that I didn't require the privilege of leading the convoy, thank you so much.

This went back and forth for awhile until they finally gave up and let us go in the middle of the convoy. This led to my being awake throughout the predawn hours negotiating. But at least I didn't have to wake up my team, other than my combat systems officer and sea detail officer of the deck and navigator, who did the actual radio negotiating with me.

We were under way at 0600, and I felt very rocky. I've been sick off and on for a week—the combination of Persian Gulf near-combat stress, the long underway days without any sleep, and excitement over getting home. This morning, I had several terrible bouts of vertigo that had me sitting in my chair hoping it would pass—bad dizziness. My head felt full of fluid. The corpsman initially diagnosed the onset of a cold and gave me an antihistamine.

As had been the case headed in, the pilots shuffled on and off, we worked our way into the canal, and we were settled into the convoy. The desert clipped by, mile after mile. I felt worse and called the "doc" back. He agreed it sounded like a real sinus infection and prescribed antibiotics and a decongestant, which I took around 1600.

In the intervening hours, we had a barbecue, let an Egyptian vendor sell on the mess decks, had the "300-pound bench pressing competition," whatever that was—something the master chief orchestrated. To say the least, I wasn't a contestant! I sat in my chair, mile after mile, hour after hour, slightly dizzy, sick, and tired—and read the fifty first-class evaluations my XO had prepared. Smile, Jim, you're headed home!

Believe me, by the time the sun was setting and Port Said, the northern port, was in sight, I was ready to break out into the open sea.

As I sit here writing this, with a two-day beard, still slightly sick, the ship is rocketing along at twenty-five knots, headed for an underway replenishment tomorrow and ultimately a quick port visit to Rota, Spain.

I hope that the "doc's" medicine will kick in, the UNREP will go smoothly, and we will have a good port visit in Rota before heading home.

In the meantime, I am simply happy to have survived the canal and put my northbound transit behind me.

120

So much has happened in the last five days.

Physical condition first. I've had a bad bout of vertigo, coming and going for nearly four days. Is it stress related? Perhaps, but I suspect it is more likely a combination of sinus pressure, low resistance, and the constant grinding motion of the ship.

It leaves me functional, but much disturbed in spirit and balance. Everything in the distance seems to "drift" just a bit in my field of vision. I've had two or three other episodes over the past twenty years, the first being, I think, when I was an ensign in California in the late 1970s. My guess is that it is all related to the bad sinus problems I had as a child. In any event, it is controllable with antihistamines, which dry me out and leave me woozy and dozy but at least not totally off balance.

That has gradually improved over the previous four days and now seems virtually gone—and that, of course, is the best news.

We left the canal at dusk, cranking up to twenty-five knots and blowing by the anchored merchants awaiting their southbound transit on the following day. I crashed hard and awoke the next morning—after perhaps forty phone calls through the night—to the large oiler *Platte* ahead of us and looking to get us alongside.

We got through that fairly routine UNREP easily, among the best I've seen at sea, including both fuel and cargo.

Then we cracked on to twenty-seven knots and powered our way to Rota.

On the way, we stopped for an hour just south of Sicily to "catch up" with the *Cape St. George*, my old friend, Al Fraser's, ship. He was just coming into the Med and was full of energy and ideas, as he always is—wanted to bring the ships to all stop and come over for a "turnover."

We changed it into a helo flight over, and he, his OPS officer, and his supply officer all came for a visit. Some great photo opportunities—it was perhaps the finest sunset of the cruise—and he and his ship seem to be doing well. Al is always full of life and good humor and has become such a good friend over the course of the twenty years I've known him. He was my exec when I was a department head—operations officer—in the *Valley Forge*. His wife, Sheila, is a delight, and the two of them are as close a friends as Laura and I have in the Navy or in life. So it was wonderful to see him and we had a thoroughly pleasant visit.

Next was the Strait of Gibraltar at dawn. A spectacular, brooding dawn—heavy, wet fog, drizzle, heavy shipping, the rock looming over our starboard hand. A British destroyer flashing us with respect as we passed. And then we were gone, out of the Med, and the cruise, save only the homecoming voyage, suddenly and smoothly complete. Can this be real?

121

Approaching the coast of Spain, we eased to fifteen knots and puttered to the entrances to Rota Naval Station. Again the dizziness threatened to overtake me, but it cleared enough to get me through the landing. Fortunately, we had the same excellent harbor pilot we'd enjoyed on the in-chop visit—an ex-boatswain mate, nice, slow touch with the ship. We turned to starboard and backed to the slip. An easy landing, and I let my ensign conning officer and sea and anchor detail OOD do most of the work. I confined myself to a couple of comments as we backed, shifting the rudder to the correct side and chiding them a little for drifting forward when we closed the pier. All in all, a smooth landing.

Then I called Laura, watched CNN, and went to dinner with the wardroom for a traditional "end of cruise" meal at La Argentina, the excellent beef house we'd hit on the way into the Med. I had a fine steak, marinated in Argentinean olive oil, vinegar, and pepper and some sautéed vegetables—tomatoes, eggplant, onion, peppers. A couple of beers, a glass of wine, and then "back ship."

We left Rota, entered the Atlantic, and immediately began to pitch harder than we had throughout the entire cruise.

122

The strong northwest winds were coming from a hurricane that had only a day before had its "closest point of approach" to our planned track. It was headed north to England, but it clearly wanted to be sure we knew it was about. The long, long, powerful swells threw the ship about like a toy. It was a hard day and night for most of the crew, many of whom had had far too much to drink in Rota the night before.

Yet dawn comes, as it always does, and the seas, though strong, began to become tolerable. People adjusted, and the routines of the ship began slowly to conquer the pitching and rolling of the sea.

123

Now it is our second day out of Rota, and we are scheduled for yet another difficult underway replenishment with the carrier. I am tired of coming alongside the carrier. The admiral watches, so many faces, the chances of a problem greater because of the pressures and presence of so many not involved in day-to-day underway replenishment. Not my choice, but here I go again—on the stage again.

I hope that this one will be as smooth as the others, and will be the last.

I really am ready to go home. It has been a long cruise.

124

The UNREP was very, very smooth. I had my best guys up there, and they did a super job.

And that, I think, is that. No more UNREPS, no more tough seamanship situations—just a long pull home.

As the days go by, the ship draws closer and closer to Norfolk, moving across the big screens in the CIC.

It is a slow time. Every minute takes longer than it should. I pass the time with books and postdeployment briefings and postexercise reports. The crew is happy, quiet, and upbeat.

In many ways I cannot believe the cruise is coming to an end. I remember going out to sea for the very first time, on a cruiser a long time ago as a midshipman at Annapolis, and listening to a junior officer I was standing watch with on the bridge, who said, "When I'm ashore, there are times I never want to go out to sea again; but when I'm at sea, especially for a long time, there are moments when I never want to return to land."

The sea is a monastery of sorts. Six months ago, I entered the monastery, and now my time as a novitiate is coming to a close. The doors to this particular monastery are about to swing open.

I know what is waiting for me—a beautiful wife, two pretty daughters, a new dog (a basset hound named Emma, for God's sake), a fine house on the water. But for many of my Sailors, there is not much, literally and figuratively, awaiting them on a rainy pier in Norfolk.

My wardroom is not thinking of this. They are wrapped up in their own lives and their own missions. And I'm trying to encourage them to think of their people and especially those who have nothing awaiting them on the pier.

125 *Home at Last!*

But the homecoming day itself was the worst weather I've seen in almost twenty years at sea—hurricane Gordon ripping unexpectedly up the coast, huge seas of twenty to forty feet, dense fog—really the very worst ever.

Yet, no weather yet invented by God can spoil a homecoming.

After six months, day for day, my crew was so ready to come home that it was a palpable feeling through the ship in the final days. And so, even though the weather was atrocious, we were ready and happy to see—albeit through miserable fog, drizzle, and harsh rain at times—Chesapeake light on the horizon.

I walked up to the bridge at six in the morning, and the ship was rolling in a harsh beam sea. I hadn't slept much because of the wild motion, and it wasn't getting any better. The radios were crackling with portents of doom—not enough tugs, the seas too high to bring the carrier in, weather getting worse for the next two days—and my heart sank.

We continued to shape our course toward the sea buoy, but my feeling was that we wouldn't get in. At best, we would be pulled in early to avoid the rapidly closing weather, but that would be a chancy run at best.

A submarine in our battle group, also returning from cruise, called us and wanted to close within a mile and tail us into port because of the terrible weather. They have trouble navigating in high seas. I told him to close no closer than three thousand yards—a mile and a half. All we need is a collision this morning, I thought to myself.

By 0800 the admiral had made his decision. We would close the formation to about eight thousand yards between the ships and press into port at best speed. That would put us alongside about 1100, about three hours early and no doubt a challenge for the wives and dependents who had been planning on the 1400 arrival for weeks. Oh, well.

At 1000 it seemed we had worked our way through the worst of it. Not surprisingly, as we moved up the narrow channel and pressed inland from the sea, the winds abated slightly to around "only" forty knots—still deadly difficult shiphandling. Still terrible, but survivable in a landing, I hope. No matter what, I'm taking her in, short of a direct order to the contrary from the admiral. I had taken the deck at one point, something rare for a captain to do, but I wanted to let my officer of the deck, Lt. Cdr. Fred Pffirrmann, make a phone call to his wife, who was pregnant. I ended up simply keeping the conn for most of the way home.

Eventually, we could see the piers ahead, with the ship in front of us, the *Thomas S. Gates*, an Aegis-class cruiser, trying to make the pier with four tugs clustered around her. She missed her first shot and was pulled back into the harbor, so we had to slow dramatically and wait in the heavy winds and currents.

I was very glad to see the pilot aboard, and he quickly brought three tugs to bear, one forward, one aft, and one midships. I hadn't had three tugs on a ship I was handling since driving the *Forrestal*, an aircraft carrier, in the late 1970s! Fortunately, they held us smoothly as we navigated the turn into the slip. My best conning officer, Lt. Terry Mosher, had the deck, and the wind was blowing us fiercely down on the pier. We "bet the bow" on the forward tug's line—something I truly did not want to do but had to—and we bounced once hard and settled to the pier.

The bridge cleared out quickly as the crew went below to meet their friends and family.

I remained behind on the bridge for a few minutes while the brow was maneuvered into place.

I thought of the day we had left, six months earlier, of Ireland and D-day. I thought of Cannes, the whirl and magic of being a captain in a faraway and glamorous place. I thought of the Persian Gulf, the sprint through the canal, the dizziness that plagued me on the return voyage, the result, I think, of simple exhaustion and strain. I thought of the long hours in the hot Adriatic summer, and the trips to foreign ships, and the challenge of air strikes, and the sense of a terrible war being fought thirty miles inland.

And then I realized, in one sweet moment, that my goals in life, in the Navy, for my country, had all fused and been achieved. There are few feelings in life, I am convinced, better than bringing a good ship home from a long voyage, with all hands healthy and happy, the mission done, and the lines firmly tying you to the pier.

And on my quiet bridge, a place I had spent so many hours for the past six months, I looked around and smiled and laughed out loud, a smile and a laugh of pure joy.

Then I walked back behind the signal bridge, down the exterior ladders, and to the quarterdeck to meet my beautiful wife and daughters, opening the door again to the real part of my world that had been missing for six long months.

What a sweet, sweet moment in a life.

126

Now it begins again—the cycle of deployment preparations.

After the initial shock of being home again wore off, we began to focus on the final challenge of the year—the maintenance and supply inspection that in Navy parlance is known as the Logistics Management Assessment (supply inspection) and 3M (for maintenance).

We had been preparing for LMA/3M for eight months, since a very poor job on an assist visit in the early spring. I had then a sense that we needed a great deal of time to get ready to achieve what I knew we could, and so we scheduled the inspection for the final week before stand down, the second week in December.

It had not been a popular decision on the ship, because it meant we would have to come back from cruise and go right into preparations for this big inspection. There was very little time, other than a quick Thanksgiving holiday, to relax before wrapping up the year.

But I knew that we could stay focused and use the time between Thanksgiving and the inspection to really do a good job. My exec was on board with the idea, as was the supply officer, Lt. Tim Morgan. The other department heads and the 3M coordinator were not happy, but I knew that once the decision was made, they would have to support it—and they did.

We began the week after Thanksgiving with an assist visit and found we had made a great deal of progress since the spring. We had completely automated the maintenance system on board, becoming the first ship to completely computerize the system. Next, we had tightened up all our logistic and supply procedures considerably, notably through the excellent work of a new chief petty officer who had reported aboard in the early summer, a tough Panamanian with extensive experience at the type commander's supply shop.

Finally, I laid out a challenge to the department heads to "validate all vulnerable checks," meaning a meticulous checking of all the possible checks the inspectors could look at. An enormous task for them, but necessary.

Why was this inspection so important?

As I told the crew, over and over, LMA/3M was the "last brick in the wall." If we did well, we would win the Battle E and all departmental awards. If not, we would really diminish all the other accomplishments of 1994, which I had come to think of as "The Year of the *Barry.*"

127

The week of the inspection was hard.

As I've mentioned before, in all Navy inspections (and all inspections, I suppose), there are moments when you are sure you are hitting the ball out of the park. And there are moments when you are sure you have failed. This was no exception.

Initial reports were good, but some of the inspectors I saw looked tired, cranky, and coldly efficient.

Then we supposedly flunked a DC spot check, a procedure where an off-ship inspector watches the crew member do a particularly important maintenance procedure. (It was later resolved in our favor.)

Then we heard they thought we were doing great.

But then the chief inspecting the galley wouldn't tell us how it was going.

Back and forth. As I told the department heads during the daily debriefs, there is a rhythm to all of this, and we just needed to keep a very steady strain on the line.

128

The debrief was dazzling. I couldn't believe the words I was hearing: "Top score in twenty-five years. An Atlantic Fleet record. Spit-shined crew members. The best engineering department on the waterfront. The best, the best, the best. . . ."

The commodore put out a message that was an amazing tribute to the crew, as did the type commander.

The ball didn't go out of the park, it bounced off the moon and turned into a comet. Where does all this come from? I just "show up and read the message traffic." It truly is an excellent wardroom, a solid crew top to bottom, and, most important in my view, the best chiefs' mess in history. They have now been together pushing four years. Unlike the officers, who have now turned over almost completely from the precommissioning wardroom, the chiefs' mess is essentially the original issue on the ship. They refuse to let anything fail; in fact, they refuse to let anything happen that doesn't set a record. Truly amazing. Chiefs really are the backbone of the seagoing Navy.

It was a good way to end the year.

129   Vision 95

As the *Barry* wrapped up 1994, I looked back on truly a fine full year in command—a great deployment, D-day, excellent liberty ports, the Adriatic, the Persian Gulf, the Golden Anchor (the award for top reenlistment, very important), the NEY award (best food in the fleet), the great LMA/3M inspection. . . .

But now it is time to turn to the new year, to create a unifying vision for the ship that will carry the *Barry* forward through the next shift in the cycle: Vision 95.

I have seen the Senate, and they were pleased.

What a month January has been. After finishing the big supply and maintenance inspection, we motored the ship up the York River, through the toughest sea detail on the East Coast, and landed at the Naval Weapons Station Yorktown. There we took the weapons off, shell by shell, missile by missile, and bullet by bullet.

During that week, I was called for a surprise "opportunity to excel" to Washington to testify in front of the Senate Armed Services Committee on readiness. Quite an experience—me at the "Joe McCarthy–style" table, microphone before me, listening and answering questions for two hours from Senators Thurmond, Nunn, Warner, McCain, Cohen, Santorum, Lieberman, Exxon, and Robb. Dangerous ground, difficult waters. While I wanted the ship to look good, the real thrust of the testimony was that the crew was tired after 70 to 75 percent out of homeport steaming for two full years after commissioning.

I received no guidance other than the simple words, "Tell the truth, tell it like it is," from Admiral Natter. Talk about leeway!

It was indeed an interesting experience. I was on a panel with three other midgrade commanders—an Air Force fighter squadron CO, an Army battalion commander, and a Marine regimental commander. All of them seem to have been selected based on their height (tall), excellent executive hair (superb), and rock hard jaws. As by far the shortest and most follicle challenged, I just tried to look sincere, which I am. The questions were fairly straightforward: How much time was your ship under way over the past year? How does the crew do with the extended separation from their family? Is the military overtaxed or overstressed? What kinds of missions are you called on to perform? I tried to stay "in my lane" and only talk about facts pertaining to my ship and my schedule. I did not venture any opinions about OPTEMPO (operational tempo; i.e., how much of their time are units forward deployed). I did say the morale on my ship was high, which it is, in my personal opinion and in the opinion of my command leadership.

Anyway, it seemed to go well, and I received good reviews—including letters from Admiral Natter expressing the CNO's and secretary of the Navy's approval over the testimony—a relief, to say the least.

After spending two days—with a car breakdown—in D.C., I blasted down to Yorktown and drove the ship back around to Norfolk, this time not back to the naval station, but into a tiny shipyard, Moon Engineering.

Moon is a little "bicycle shop" in Navy parlance, that is to say a small yard. Only two hundred full-time employees, only two thirds the size of my crew, but they are to work a wide variety of jobs all over my destroyer.

They seem willing, if a little inexperienced, at this point. The yard is run by two brothers, Jimmy and Wayne Thomas, who seem competent and very interested in providing a quality yard period to us. Their team is not polished, but they seem extremely well intentioned and motivated.

The only hard part was physically getting the ship into the yard. The water is very shallow, they used commercial tugs and a Virginia harbor pilot (i.e., not the highly competent Navy tugs and pilots), and the wind was blowing over forty-five knots, with two knots of current running. We ended up with the ship canted out around the corner of the pier, fended off by the largest tug.

After a lot of jockeying, we finally managed to get pushed into a very narrow slip, with only a few feet between us and the enormous roll-on/roll-off ship across the slip at the only other pier in the "yard."

Since then, we've been stringing cable, running latticelike supports up the sides of the ship for scaffolding, and settling into the hated "industrial environment," read DIRTY.

We are fighting the good fight, but day by day the ship is filling with grit and grime, the presence of the yard workers bears down, and the sense of a perfectly squared-away destroyer is replaced by an industrial hulk under control of the yard.

We are fighting, fighting, fighting—but the real solution is saltwater and underway time in the spring. . . .

131

What can I say about being in a shipyard, besides I hate it?

Fortunately, in a week we'll be under way again.

We've only been in the yards for nine weeks, but it feels like forever. The good news is that I can see the cables lifting and retreating from the ship, the yard workers fewer in number, the jobs wrapping up, and yes, with some luck, we'll be smoothly under way a week from today.

I've asked the navigator to review all the charts and tides and currents with me. It has been a good while since we've driven the ship to sea—almost three months—and we all need to dust the cobwebs out of our collective minds.

As captain, my preparations are more personal. I'll review shiphandling, rules of the road, watch bills, engineering preparations, sea trial schedules, and a host of other potential "cracks" in the great wall of preparations my team has been building.

The other big change is the arrival of women in the crew!

As I heard through the rumor mill some months ago, the Navy made a decision to send women to destroyers, and the *Barry* is the first of this class to embark female Sailors.

They will make up between 10 and 15 percent of the crew after all arrive and are roughly 10 percent as we depart the yards. Their numbers include three division officers (all three classmates from Annapolis, interestingly), a department head (our new supply officer), three chief petty officers (including an imposing senior chief boatswain mate), and about twenty-five E-6 and below.

I've spent lots of time talking to the families of our Sailors and to our male crew members about why this is a good thing for the *Barry* and important to the Navy.

My emphasis is on the quality of the women, the necessity of using all Sailors to crew all our ships, and on our policy to avoid either fraternization or harassment of any of our new shipmates. As I tell the male crew members, their new shipmates aren't coming here to date them, but rather to stand shoulder to shoulder with them in a ship of war.

About three weeks after the first women checked aboard, all of the male crew members sort of looked around and shrugged and said, "What was all the fuss about?" Our new shipmates are doing fine, and I'm not too worried about the mixed gender character of the ship. In fact, I notice people tend to act a little less rough around the edges, swearing has been reduced significantly, and there is just a good all-around tone in the command. We'll probably have a few pregnancies along the way, but, hey, we have guys with back and knee problems too, and every other sort of issue. My guess is the vast majority of the women will be excellent shipmates, in roughly the same talent proportion as their male counterparts. And its not like this is the first SHIP in the Navy to have women; we've had women at sea in Navy ships for two decades, just not in the smaller crew confines of a destroyer.

All will be well.

The biggest preparatory inspection is the light-off assessment, which we are just completing. A team of seven fairly experienced midgrade engineers—both officer and senior enlisted—from our destroyer squadron comes over and goes through every aspect of our engineering plant, from safety checks to administrative programs, and gives us a "safe to steam" certification.

We are also doing lots of safety preparations, and I'll be talking to the entire crew over the 1MC during our coming "fast cruise." A fast cruise is a full day spent pretending to be at sea while still tied to the pier. My plan is to actually get into the ship's rigid inflatable boat (RHIB) and cruise up and down the channel refreshing my seaman's eye and seeing where the dredges are located in the channel now. We almost hit one coming in here, and I'd just as soon have a smoother transit out to sea next Monday.

Am I nervous?

Well, nothing like first getting the ship under way eighteen months ago when I first took command. We'll simply glide out of this pier here (although it is very closely packed in) and motor on down the long channel to the sea—about a three-hour drive.

But despite seventy thousand nautical miles in command under my belt, I am still a little nervous, I discover as I monitor my internal feelings. I guess it stems from several things. First of all, I wonder whether my and the crew's skills have atrophied to a significant degree while our ship has been here in the yards. I think we'll be OK there, because we haven't been in all that long. Second, I'm concerned about the machines—the steering and engines. One of them failing at a critical time could present a very real problem. And we'll practice our responses to emergencies like that as we do the fast cruise, so I think we'll be ready there. Third, we'll have lots of new crew members, including our first female shipmates. The new faces will bring up some challenges I'm sure as people readjust to the presence of so many new shipmates. But again, we are training and rehearsing, and I think everyone should have a pretty good idea of what they need to do and where they should be. So, hopefully that will be OK. Lastly, I suppose the ship's very strong reputation intimidates me a little. We have done so well thus far that it would be very, very sad to have a failure here close to the end.

I remember Kevin Greene, now a destroyer squadron commander on the West Coast, telling me that "your first six months will be the most uncomfortable, the last three the most dangerous." I am starting Monday on the last six or so months of my tour, and I just don't know how it will come out. I'd hate to blow it at the end.

Yet, you always have to remain philosophical. All you can do is the best you can do, and I will try to think through all that can happen in this first under way after two months in the yards and hopefully anticipate any problems before they emerge. With preparation, luck, God's help, and our own true eye we should be just fine.

132

The awards have been coming in rather steadily. We won the Battle Efficiency E, the *only* guided missile destroyer on the East Coast to do so—de facto the top DDG in the Atlantic Fleet. We also won the four departmental awards—supply, engineering, seamanship/operations, combat systems. We won the Ney Award as the top food service ship in the Atlantic Fleet—a personal priority. And best of all, we are the squadron nominee for the Battenberg Cup as the best ship in the Atlantic Fleet. Whether we win or not doesn't really matter. The nomination means we are the best of seventeen ships in the squadron.

On a personal side, I was the runner-up for the John Paul Jones Award of the Navy League, the *Proceedings* author of the year, and a finalist for the Admiral Stockdale Award, which requires nomination by a peer.

It has been a good year—1994—indeed.

I suppose an operative question is why are we winning these awards? Several reasons:

- Lucky schedule. We deployed in the heart of the window for all the awards, returning from a very successful deployment to Haiti, Bosnia, and the Gulf just as the cycle ended.

- Superb chiefs' mess. Best I've ever seen; they give the wardroom the time and space to concentrate on the "nice to have" touches in terms of creative operations, postexercise messages, ideas for improvement. They do the basic blocking and tackling, freeing up the officers to do the things that make the ship stand out.
- A few superstars. People like Terry Mosher, who invents new training programs; Vince McBeth, who develops new ways to approach air control; Tim Morgan, who designs the most creative cycle menu in the history of food service; and countless others.
- Good humor. The command climate is the most free of fear and intimidation I've ever seen. That it is so is a tribute to the combined efforts of the entire crew, who have collectively decided that this will be the ship where no one loses their temper or belittles others.
- Having a plan (or lots of plans). Everything is done with a written-down, responsibilities-assigned, accountable dates sort of process, driven by the executive officer and department heads.
- Luck. No ship does this well without simply being lucky. I always say there is a rainbow around the *Barry*, and this run tends to prove it.

So a good year.

But this is no time to sit back and feel good. Now it is time to turn with renewed energy and focus on 1995, to build a ship that will sail safely and professionally in a new battle group long after I am gone. The question now is: How to build on success to get to even another level.

133

We won the Battenberg Cup.

It is hard to describe how important this is to the crew and to the ship. The award dates back decades and is awarded annually, simply, to the "best ship in the Atlantic Fleet." Winning it makes the *Barry* the best of well over 150 ships. It is amazing for a destroyer to win it, as it is normally carried off by an aircraft carrier or a cruiser—a far larger ship, commanded by a more experienced and sensible officer than the captain of our relatively tiny destroyer.

The messages, letters, and general accolades pour in—from around the world, quite literally. Classmates from Annapolis, people I haven't heard from in years, admirals—everyone in the Navy circuit—they all send kind words.

The announcement comes on the heels of a visit to Annapolis for graduation in late May, followed by a stop in Baltimore's Inner Harbor. The Baltimore visit is slightly marred by the worst landing I've executed in my entire career. I let a young, bright officer—one of our new women—drive the ship. She is a reasonably good shiphandler, but the landing was challenging, the pilot and tugs ridiculously bad, and I simply let it get too far before I stepped in. We ended up banging the stern on the pier, putting a small dent in it, and were only saved at the end game by the stern safety officer— Lt. Russ Wycoff, a brilliant former enlisted combat systems officer—making an on-scene decision to shoot lines over and winch the stern in. Later, surveying the damage, my laconic XO, Mike Franken said, "Forget it, Captain. That's why they give you extra paint." We painted it up and will bang the dents out back in Norfolk. A curious counterpoint to being named the "best ship in the Atlantic Fleet." Still, I'll take the cup and the dent as a package, I guess.

One sad note. A friend and mentor of mine, Rear Adm. Jay Prout, died suddenly and shockingly last week. He was flying in a Hornet across country, coincidentally with a classmate of mine, Joe Kleefish, piloting the aircraft. Joe evidently became disoriented, and they crashed in the side of a mountain. So, so sad. Jay was a bright, funny, engaging officer of amazing potential. He and his wife, Kathy, have been truly nice to me and Laura over the years. Jay was unquestionably on his way to the very top of the Navy, having just been selected for a second star and in command of Cruiser-Destroyer Group Three on the West Coast when all this happened.

I sent Kathy a note:

Dear Kathy,

I sat last night on the bridge of *Barry* and thought of Jay. It was an early summer night in the Caribbean, warm and breezy. The stars stretched on forever.

He was a remarkable man, and I am lucky to have known him. I saw him last just over a week ago in Norfolk, at a Navy party, drinking beer in his whites, laughing with Bob Natter, Phil Coady, and other friends. We talked for half an hour about Coronado, and the Battle Group and about you and the children. Jay was very happy, full of friendship and light and good ideas. I remember thinking when we said good-bye how much I enjoyed talking to him and how lucky we were to have him in the Navy.

Kathy, with all my heart I wish this had not happened. If there is anything—today or forever—that I can do for you or the children, call on me.

Laura and our girls join me in extending our deepest sympathy. To know the love of God is to know eternity. Jay will be with us always.

134

Into each command tour, a few setbacks must fall.

After all the awards, and all the kudos, after the Battenberg Cup, the Oscar of ship awards, we have failed a big test.

As I write this, we have suffered the toughest setback of my twenty-one months in command. After repairing the electronic casualty of last week, we returned to port well ready for the big engineering inspection. We cleaned the ship and the engineering plant, rested the crew over the weekend, and greeted the inspectors, the Propulsion Examining Board (PEB), at the quarterdeck on Tuesday morning at 0800.

The senior inspector has a reputation as a tough, loud, abrasive, domineering officer. Six foot six, a former amphibious ship commanding officer (with a bit of a chip on his shoulder toward destroyers and cruisers, some on the waterfront say) and lifelong engineer, he had been alternatively described to me as "tough but fair" and "an unfair tyrant, out to flunk everyone."

I met him at the quarterdeck, where he (of course) towered over me and everyone else. He seemed friendly enough, although he was loud.

We toured the spaces together and, I thought, hit it off fairly well. He seemed knowledgeable and focused on safety issues: heat, fuse boxes (electricity), cleanliness.

His team then went through our admin programs. This is the first step in a big engineering inspection, which essentially has four key parts—the administrative (paperwork) review of all our deck-level programs; material inspection for safety, essentially a thorough look through the plant; operations under way, which are closely observed; a series of drills (practice sessions), where our ability to respond to casualties and to train ourselves are studied; and a damage control review, culminating with a practice main-space fire, considered the most dangerous casualty a ship can face at sea.

Of our twelve administrative programs, five were excellent, five were merely satisfactory, and two—hearing conservation and heat stress—were unsatisfactory. The two unsatisfactory programs were the only two evaluated by the senior inspector. My team was much incensed by their view that he went into the reviews with a very aggressive, "you're all screwed up," attitude. There is an appeal process for the administrative programs, so I wasn't too concerned at this point, but it seemed an inauspicious beginning, and it certainly bore out the darker side of the comments I'd been hearing. Hmmmmm.

Later that day, as we headed out to sea, the lube oil in the main reduction gear began to cloud up. Lube oil is the lifeblood of the engineering plant (just like in your car), as it allows the huge engines to turn safely and smoothly. If it is dirty, it loses its lubricating powers and the ship must stop at sea. If you lose both of your engines, you will be towed ignominiously back to port. Even a bit of cloudiness was disturbing, although we have lube oil purifiers (cleaners) that can scrub the oil clean in most situations.

But in our case, by midafternoon, instead of being clear and bright, the oil had turned milky and yellow. We did everything we were supposed to, including stopping and locking the shaft. That night we set the purifiers on it, hoping it would clear up overnight.

When I woke up, the first thing I did was call the engineering officer of the watch, Petty Officer Darwin, and ask about the lube oil. "Still cloudy, sir." The bottom fell out of my stomach.

We tried the rest of the day to purify the oil, finally shifting our approach to simply dumping the oil in the sump (the big storage tank of some eighteen hundred gallons) and refilling with new, pure oil. We had enough fresh oil onboard to do this exactly once—after that we were "out of beer." By this time, we thought we found the problem—the purifier itself.

After dumping all the oil and refilling, a six-hour process, we thought we'd be ready to go with drills. I went confidently down into the space to meet my senior chief "oil king," who was tapping a sample of the fresh new oil off the sump. I was supremely confident it would be fine and we'd be off and running. After all, this was the *Barry*—the ship that sailed under the rainbow.

He ran the bottle full from the sample tap and held it up to the light. It was as milky and obviously as contaminated as all the previous samples!

Clearly, we had a bigger problem.

135

We reassessed the situation. We sampled the effluent coming from the purifiers. It was now salty, indicating a salt water leak into the oil. Truly bad news, and a new clue. Now only one place, the lube oil cooler itself, could be the source of the problem.

That meant, effectively, the end of the exam.

There was nothing left to do but return to port. The inspection team refused to conduct drills on the unaffected shaft, an option they could have taken, but simply refused to do so. Their authority in such situations was absolute.

So, the inspection was ungraded, technically "terminated without finding." While this is better than out-and-out flunking the exam, it sure feels like failure to me.

We limped back into port on our unaffected shaft (we have two, and the contamination was fortunately confined to one side only). It was a dark, windy, and cold night for that time of year. The pilot who swung aboard made sympathetic noises, and I sat in my chair on the bridge wing as we rounded the buoys, one by one, leading back to Norfolk. The mood was dark indeed, darker even than the moonless night.

By the next morning, a determined, almost angry mood settled on the crew. As I walked the ship throughout the morning hours, people were grim faced but very, very determined. They wanted the casualty fixed and a chance to get back to sea and restore the ship's reputation. The waterfront was certainly up to speed on the casualty, and I received a dozen phone calls from fellow captains offering sympathy and advice. The commodore and his staff swung into action, and all the resources of the port were turned to our disposal to effect the repairs. The retake of the exam was set up for a couple of weeks later, although I kept insisting we wanted to get back to sea within a few days.

We spent a frantic week in port, cleaning the entire lube oil system. Yes, eight tubes were broken (out of two hundred) inside the lube oil cooler. A stunning, inexplicable, and truly terrible stroke of luck. The fault, like a congenital flaw in a human heart, was hidden deep in the guts of the engineering plant, probably implanted years earlier when the cooler was landing on its site in the building yard.

We plugged the tubes. We hydroed (water pressure tested) the lube oil cooler. We flushed and filled, all weekend, with heart-stoppingly milky samples off the first two flush and fills. But by Monday the sample was clear, and we were cleared to recommence the inspection.

All that we had done—the Battenberg Cup as the top ship in the Atlantic Fleet, which had been announced as ours just a few weeks earlier; the Ney Award as the top "feeder" in the fleet; the Battle E as the top ship in the squadron; all departmental awards, the Thompson Trophy for excellence—the reputation that brought all of that to us now was hanging in the balance.

If we went forth and knocked the ball out of the park on the concluding portion of OPPE, we would be OK. We would, in the words of Admiral Giffen, our new battle group commander, survive this. Hardly a comforting turn of phrase, but his assessment was honest.

137

Well, the OPPE is over, and it has been a draining experience.

We sailed on OPPE II (if you will) on a Tuesday, planning on a couple of days to complete the items remaining in the inspection—casualty control drills, the main-space fire drill, and the full power run. I think we are ready.

The same angry commander returned, bringing with him the new head of the PEB, a full captain.

The captain seemed like a reasonable, nice, and balanced individual, but that impression was to change over the next forty-eight hours.

It started badly and didn't get better. The lube oil was still a slight bit cloudy, and everyone was very on edge about that. Still, we were able to convince the board that we were ready to start drills, after several other missteps, including a poorly filled-out heat stress form by what turned out to be a dyslexic Sailor.

I won't belabor the experience because it doesn't deserve it. We did well on the drills, quite well on the main-space fire drill, and extremely well on the full power run.

We were given a "satisfactory" across the board. Although I would have preferred higher grades, I was satisfied. I think the first week's experience left a poor impression, despite the fact that the casualty had been a sort of "act of God" beyond the control of the crew, and we weren't able to overcome that. So we "escape" with a SAT, and it is on to the next challenge.

Overall it was a deeply disappointing moment, and yet, as the XO said to me with a wink in his eye, "Best SAT ever, Captain." My new XO, Mike Franken, is a real gem. A big, raw-boned Iowa farm boy, he is as steady and sure an officer as I've ever set eyes on. A fine athlete, he is equally at home sinking a thirty-foot jump shot as he is driving the ship in bad weather. I'm lucky to have him as a running mate. A good XO—like Charlie Martoglio, my first; Ben Goslin, my second; or Mike Franken, third and final—can be a real savior to a captain. When things haven't gone too well, it's the XO who can help you square your shoulders and get the ship sailing fair again. Mike sure does that for me. There can't be a more important relationship in the armed forces than a captain and his second in command at sea, and I've been lucky with all three execs over the course of this tour.

Anyway, the big engineering inspection has come and gone. Let's see what comes next.

138

It turned out to be a hurricane. Geez.

The week after the engineering inspection was terrible because of the hectic needs of the home front. We were moving out of our house and into a small hotel on the beachfront for the week, and it was the worst move we've had—surly, incompetent movers, 100-degree weather, a bug infestation in our goods, a thousand other problems.

Then it was time to go on leave, a chance to unwind after the OPPE. I put Laura and the girls on a plane to Florida to spend a week, ahead of me, with her parents. Then I flew down myself on a Saturday morning.

I spent the day getting settled and playing a quick couple of sets of tennis with Hank Baltar, one of my oldest friends. Then I took Laura and my visiting sister Ann out to see a movie.

When I walked back in the door, there was a message to call my XO, Mike Franken.

"Captain, we've been put into hurricane condition V, which means forty-eight-hour notice to get under way." He added some details about the storm, which was well over a thousand miles away, south of Bermuda. I told him to keep an eye on it, and we'd talk on Sunday. I reassured Laura that, no, there wasn't any burning need to return.

Ten minutes later the phone rang again.

"Captain, XO here. Bad news. We are sailing tomorrow at noon. I'll get the ship under way and go to anchorage near the piers across the river, and we'll await your arrival before sailing out to sea."

So, there you have it. Eighteen hours into my vacation, recalled to the ship. I borrowed my dad's older Volvo and flew up highway 95, traveling 710 miles in under nine hours (I figured I had a good story for a police officer), and caught the ship at the pier, where our sailing was delayed while the flag officers pondered the storm track.

Off we went for hurricane evasion, which is a traditional move on the part of the Navy—get the ships out of port, where they can be trapped in the path of a devastating storm, and let them use their speed and maneuverability to dodge away from the hurricane out in the deep Atlantic.

139

The pondering went on for two days, as my vacation days burned away down in Florida. We finally sailed on Tuesday at first light, with CNN and the local networks filming the *Barry* as we lifted effortlessly off the side of the cruiser *Normandy* and motored into a morning sun as big and as red as I've ever seen.

By midday, we were in serious seas, rocking and rolling badly, with about a third of the crew down with sea sickness and the rest tired, upset, and shaken.

We have weathered the first twenty-four hours at sea and still have no idea when we'll return. I'd guess seven days, but it largely depends on what the storm does. If it simply breaks up on the Carolina coast, we'll return by Saturday; if it follows the "typical" hurricane track for this region this time of the year, it will bounce off the coast, catch the Gulf Stream, gather force, and chase us way, way out into the deep Atlantic. We turned north coming out of Norfolk and haven't many good options left. We could easily be under way for two weeks.

So much for my leave this year—with ninety-two days on the books and not another realistic chance to take any between now and transferring!

140

This hurricane evasion has been the hardest cruise of my nearly two years in command.

Over three thousand nautical miles—the width of the United States—in one huge circle, dodging the hurricane and missing a long-planned vacation and my daughter's tenth birthday and a thousand other things that will never come again.

Me to my XO: "I can't believe I'm missing Christina's tenth birthday."

XO: "You won't see another one of those."

Isn't that the truth.

We've tried to fill the time with meaningless drills and exercises, but the seas have been bad, and about half the crew is seasick. Very tough to keep people interested, especially when the captain isn't very interested either.

Me to the XO: "Mike, I'm really losing interest."

XO: "Try to stay with it, Captain."

You can't even take a shower out here without falling into the shiny walls of the zinc-covered shower stalls.

When I look back on my twenty years in the Navy and try to articulate why I'm getting out, I'll think of this hurricane cruise as an epigram for the entire twenty years.

You sail not knowing why or where you are headed, steam in an enormous circle, miss a dozen things that are important and will never come again, and finally make port in a dispirited fashion, wondering what it was all about.

That, of course, is what finally happened. After our "hurricane cruise," we came stumbling home, me to an empty house, with Laura and the girls still in Florida.

It had never even rained in Norfolk—not a drop.

141

All of this leads to the largest question in my life—whether or not to stay in the Navy.

I could certainly retire next year with twenty years under my belt, a fine command tour in the bank, take my PhD, and go off to greener pastures.

I can't make up my mind, but that is nothing new. I haven't been able to make up my mind my entire life. At first I wasn't sure I wanted to go to the Naval Academy. Then I wanted to quit and leave after my second year there. And then I knew that there wasn't anything to hold me in after my initial five-year commitment. And then after graduate school, when young and married, I wanted something better, something more than the Navy offered. Now the twenty-year point looms large indeed.

There are those who think I should stay. In some ways I've led a charmed career, with several choice assignments, a fine command tour, a chance to work for and with some of the best people in the world, perhaps even the opportunity to make a difference in the security of the United States . . . and yet. And yet.

All the birthdays missed, the holidays at sea. The frustrations, the low pay, the tired tired tired nights of long watches stood on rolling decks at the end of the world. Knowing that your life was on the line in the interests of hardly who knows what for any reason at all. And yet. And yet.

The sun setting, blood red when we sortied the fleet. The danger. The liberty in cities you would never see in a thousand other lines of work, coming to know so well the best (and, sadly, sometimes the worst) of American youth working for you. The calm, serene nights with a cigar on a bridge wing. Being the captain. Being the captain.

I've got to figure out this "balance thing" everyone talks about one of these days.

At this point, my plan is to go ashore on this next tour and—as I have so often in the past—see what the Navy's next good offer on the table looks like. If it includes something truly interesting, who knows?

I might sail again at sea yet before this is all over.

This I know for sure: A long line of sea captains have walked and sailed their ships before me. And I am lucky to have had this chance to experience the sea and the people who sail it.

142

One of the women in my crew came by to see me today. Uncharacteristically tongue tied, she asked me how you would go about changing a policy in the Navy.

What is the problem, I asked.

She and her husband, another seagoing naval officer, had been talking about having a baby. Yet, where was the time to do it? Was there a program for a year of maternity leave?

No, I don't think so, I told her. But I can check on it and let you know.

She left and I wondered where we were going. The warrior mentality, the desire to have children, the need for a career. All in collision. But in this new world, we—the Navy—need to figure this one out. If we can't, I think we'll have true difficulties keeping women engaged in Navy careers, which we must do if we are going to crew the fleet as we must.

143

The swells were shocking today in their power. "Awesome" is an overused word—especially by the twenty-somethings in my crew—but they were indeed awesome to see. Twenty feet on both sides of the stern, like sheer blue walls of the darkest, richest blue, a blue kicked up by the late summer hurricanes from the very bottom of the ocean, surrounding the ship in a shifting blue fist.

God lives out in those waves.

144

A great success last week.

The *Barry* conducted the first-ever Final Evaluation Period (FEP), a tough four-day inspection designed to stress every aspect of the ship's operational capability. We did precision anchoring, emergency sortie, small boat attack, casualty-control drills, engineering drills, damage-control drills, all forms of warfare, and, most important, a cruise missile qualification, which tests the ship's ability to launch Harpoon and Tomahawk missiles.

The head inspector was truly, really, deeply a nice guy. What a change from OPPE! Tom Bennett, a Naval Academy graduate and reasonable person, made the whole experience tough yet fair, challenging yet rewarding.

There were, as always, a few heart-stopping moments, notably one where we were criticized for not launching our Tomahawk within four seconds of the assigned time. It didn't seem like that big a deal to me (after all, we're talking about a flight time in hours and motors that could easily make up the time), but Tom came on rather strongly that it could mean failure! Fortunately, we had our arguments on line and correct, and other than that one point of contention, everything else was just about perfect.

The final messages were warm and glowing, for example, "The *Barry* sails closer to the wind than all others," "most excellent FEP." Our final inspection of my tour and a good one to wrap up on.

My orders, to go to the Joint Staff in Washington to a staff position in the J-5 (Directorate of Strategy, Plans, and Policy), are "on the board." Laura and the girls are already up in a rental in the suburb of Mount Vernon, so the kids can start school.

I can't believe I'll give up command and soon be in a little cubicle, watching a computer screen, never seeing the sea and the sky coming together on the far side of a squall line. My relief has been named—Cdr. Kevin Quinn—and is "in the pipeline" inexorably headed this way.

145

Regarding the tiny and least important piece of the *Barry* equation that is me personally, I have received my final competitive fitness report, which ranked me number one of six guided-missile destroyer COs in the squadron and effectively pushes me forward to another command at sea. Should I want another command at sea.

146

We are under way again, this time for six weeks of training in the Caribbean. My irrepressible destroyer squadron commander and good friend John Morgan has put together a superb training exercise, and we are motoring south in formation with a dozen other ships, enjoying the chance to be at sea.

On the home front, I've moved Laura and the girls up to Washington and they are settling nicely into our new place.

They are enjoying themselves but cannot quite figure out why dad hasn't move up with them. I can't wait to finish up (three months to go) and join them.

147

The commodore came to visit today.

John Morgan has become one of the real constants and inspirations of my tour. He has so much energy and determination and so many ideas. It is a pleasure to be around him.

We had Mexican food in the cabin, and we toured the ship. He spoke to a group of my Sailors who are applying for a commissioning program and told them they should "go forth and do great things," quoting Abraham Lincoln. A wonderful little five-minute talk, and one those five young men and women will remember their whole lives I would guess.

And on we sail, the Southern Cross appearing nightly and beckoning my ship, on this penultimate voyage, into the warm Caribbean. Can this all be coming to a halt so soon?

148

This last trip to the Caribbean in the *Barry* has been a success thus far. As I write this, we've been under way just under a month, with a week to go before coming home. The key exercises, from my perspective, have been the anti–air warfare (AAW) drills; the naval gunfire range; and the underway replenishments.

The anti–air warfare has been superb. My team, still largely intact from last cruise, has done a great job of reestablishing the *Barry*'s reputation as a premier AAW ship. We are good on the circuits, reliable in our judgments, calm in the execution of war-fighting strategy, and a good missile shooter. We shot 3 for 3 on the range, against a mixed bag of tough targets.

The naval gunfire was the highlight of the trip. We shot the highest destroyer score in the fleet last year, a 103.5. Unfortunately, I had an entirely new team on station this year, led by a brand-new department head, Lt. Neal Ellis. They faced a tough uphill struggle and almost failed the initial gunfire qualification back in Norfolk, a classroom drill. They trained very, very hard on the way down, however, and went into the day-long actual firing qualification at Vieques Island with high hopes.

Things began poorly, with an incorrect navigation error and a casualty to the gun. Then they improved dramatically, to the degree that I thought we had a real chance of breaking 100 again with only a single exercise left to shoot. We had to delay at that point for aircraft over the range. When we returned, predictably, the gun broke again. There was a flurry of activity, but we just couldn't complete correcting the casualty and had to limp away with the exercise left to shoot.

Then, after another hour of troubleshooting, the problem was corrected by bleeding off a little of the high-pressure air that controls the big gun. We shot back to the range and talked them into letting us shoot the final exercise.

To everyone's overwhelming happiness and surprise, we shot a 103.7, beating our old record! Everyone was "styling" all over combat, as the operational specialists would say. Commodore Morgan sent several wonderful messages, among them a birthday greeting to old Adm. Arleigh Burke—still alive in the Virginian, a senior citizen's home in Northern Virginia—with the news that one of "his" ships (ours, of course, is an *Arleigh Burke*–class destroyer) shot a "perfect score" on the range. What a feeling!

It occurred to me that the gunfire range was a microcosm of the entire tour—the lowest of lows as the gun broke, the struggle to correct, the ultimate triumph and vindication, and the recognition for the crew and ship. The highs are so high and the lows are so low . . . two years is long enough. There isn't enough of me to take much more of the fire on the burner here.

The last thing that was hard and a challenge were the various graded underway replenishments. We did well enough, but the final one (I hope) was last night, and it was one worth remembering. It was a dark Caribbean evening, with no horizon and a little wind when I came on the bridge. We were in station about six hundred yards astern of the oiler, and I took a quick look around and told Terry Mosher, my sea and replenishment detail OOD, to take her in. The conning officer was Lt. Scott Bewley, my best underway replenishment OOD.

Just as we accelerated, all hell broke loose. There was suddenly fifty knots of wind across the deck, blowing rain, and a howling storm. It was a tropical microburst, the cutting edge of the worst kind of squall, and it hit just as we approached the dangerous stern area of the oiler. I think the conning team—Mosher, Bewley, and the XO—wanted to wave off but weren't saying anything. They sort of looked my way. It was a captain's moment.

I ordered all stop, just in time, and we slid back away from the underway replenishment. I called the oiler and told them my intention was to wait and clear the squall. They agreed, and we all retreated inside the bridge, watching the rain fall and the night darken. I couldn't believe the bad luck and wondered how long the storm would last.

Fortunately, it cleared in about half an hour, and the stars came out so bright they lit the horizon. It was, at the end, a beautiful, smooth night, with the water below like blue cream, the ships knifing through.

149

The final week at sea that I will have in my command tour consists of a three-day war game, led by our battle group commander, Adm. Hank Giffen. He flew in for this today, and tomorrow we'll all join him over on the carrier for a briefing. I think it will go well, and with any luck we'll be on our way to Mayport, Florida, our next port visit, by Tuesday.

150

Well, I've completed two years in command.

The crew threw me a party, complete with the largest cake I've ever seen and all hands on the mess decks for an ice cream social. This after I told the XO specifically I didn't want anything special. The wardroom also had a special dinner, with china, crystal, and the mess servers in their tuxedos. All very nice.

And what will I think of as I look back on two years in command? A message I received, from the crew, probably sums it up best:

Z 211800Z OCT 95
FROM USS BARRY
TO BARRY
BT
UNCLAS PERSONAL FOR STAVRIDIS FROM
CREW OF BARRY//N00000//
MSGID/GENADMIN/BARRY//
SUBJ/THANKS FOR TWO GREAT YEARS//
    RMKS/1. ON BEHALF OF ALL THE
OFFICERS, CHIEF PETTY OFFICERS, AND
CREW OF THE GOOD SHIP BARRY, WE
THANK YOU FOR TWO UNFORGETTABLE
YEARS.

2. FROM OUR HAITIAN VACATION, TO A ONCE-IN-A-LIFETIME CRUISE, TO THE HARBOR OF KUWAIT CITY, YOU HAVE LED US AND BARRY ALONG, AND IN SOME CASES OVER THE CUTTING EDGE TO A REPUTATION AS "BEST IN THE FLEET!" FAIR WINDS AND FOLLOWING SEAS TO A GREAT CAPTAIN.
3. ONCE AGAIN THANK YOU. YOURS, VERY RESPECTFULLY, THE CREW OF BARRY//
BT

What a ride it all has been. Two years, 113,000 miles as of this moment. An amazing run of challenges and accomplishments. The Battenberg Cup. The Ney Award. The Thompson Trophy. The Golden Anchor. The Battle E at the mast, and all the departmental awards.

Yet, all of it that matters can be found in the faces of the young men and women I've been so lucky to work with in the *Barry*. The float in my dreams, just beyond recognition, trying, trying, trying to do their very best.

Two years.

151 *The Last Under Way*

This final period at sea has been very full of emotion for me. We sailed at the end of November, after a very tough month of preparations. This final three-week exercise is the battle group's "graduation exercise" preparation for the deployment.

But let me back up.

After returning from the long five-week cruise to the Caribbean that marked two years in command, we had a hectic week in port loading ammunition. Then we sortied again for ten days with the amphibious ships.

Amphibs are the Marine-carrying, large, slow ships that need destroyer and cruiser escorts to get them safely from point A to B, quite literally from tedium to boredom in most cases.

We were under way with a cruiser, the *San Jacinto*, commanded by a big, burly, former football player from Florida named Ray Pilcher. Not one to suffer fools or boring exercises in silence, he sent me a message welcoming me to the "1950s," referring to the slow, old-fashioned pace of the amphib exercises. He said to make sure I have my saddle shoes on.

And he was right.

Slow, boring ops. The crew was tired from five weeks under way and wondering why we were out again steaming slowly at two knots ten miles off the coast of Carolina. They can watch Oprah on morning TV but can't be at home to have a cup of coffee with their wives? Makes little sense; to them or me.

Still, it is a necessary drill. If we are involved in any real-world operations this cruise, it will probably require landing Marines. So we must practice.

That finally staggered to a halt, and we returned to port for my final in-port period as CO. I was mostly taken up with going back and forth to D.C. to see Laura and the girls and preparing the ship for the change of command.

Certainly, the highlight was the going away party the wardroom threw me. Laura and I drove down for it from Washington, with her parents staying with our daughters.

It was held at my XO's house in the Norfolk suburb of Little Neck on a frosty fall night. Our commodore, John Morgan, came unexpectedly and was a wonderful addition. His presence meant a great deal to me. He spoke of all I have been able to do in the *Barry* and ended with Napoléon's quote that a "leader must be a dealer of hope." Very moving words.

My fine navigator, and really the best overall officer in the *Barry* (including me), Lt. Robb Chadwick, was also leaving. He likewise spoke very movingly of the effect I had had on the ship. He said, and I will never forget it, that the ship that sailed to Haiti (at the very start of my command tour) wasn't the ship that returned. That I had brought a sense of real-world operations to what had been a construction process before that. He said many very kind things beyond that, and I felt the warmth of the wardroom and a very real sense of sadness at my departure. It was all very moving to me.

We sailed to sea for the final voyage of my command tour on 29 November, on a cool and overcast fall day.

152

These final days are so very full emotionally, and somewhat empty operationally.

Despite the whirling fleet exercise all around us, I have not had to become terribly personally involved. My well-trained teams of four tactical action officer, four deck-watch sections—each with three well-trained teams—and four engineering officers of the watch all run the ship very nicely, with an occasional call to the captain.

We have replenished three times, each time smoothly and easily. We've had several severe casualties to the engineering plant and smoothly and easily repaired them within twenty-four hours. We have defended the carrier and the amphibious ships and have sailed close to shore and deep to sea. The weather, thus far, has been kind to us.

The crew is very happy and, I think, well adjusted to the coming change of command. I have repeatedly talked about my relief in the most glowing terms, both because he deserves it—he has a fine reputation—and because it will ease the transition. The crew is anticipating a good, new captain with his own set of initiatives and ideas. They are cautiously optimistic, and I don't think any of them really think anything bad can happen to the *Barry*. And they are right.

The officers are doing extremely well. Mike Franken, the finest exec in the Navy, has truly come into his own and is the dominant force, day to day, in the ship. Terry Mosher is the tactician and mariner. I have very deliberately pushed them forward more and more as the year has gone on to ensure the transition would go smoothly. Both are fully capable of running the ship in their worlds, and together they will make a wonderful top-level team for Kevin Quinn. The command master chief, newly arrived, is still finding his way but has his heart in the right place and I think will ultimately do a fine job for the *Barry*.

I spend my days walking the ship, remembering different adventures and dangers and delights and triumphs. There is much good to remember, and I am the luckiest captain in the world.

153

Kevin Quinn arrived today.

Medium height, a youthful face, and a quiet, pleasant manner. He was a year behind me at Annapolis, although we are the same age chronologically. I remember him as a smart, self-contained midshipman and a decent tennis player. I tried to encourage him to come out for the tennis team with me, but he focused on his grades. Fair enough.

Within a day, he is quite comfortable in the ship, walking on his own, meeting crew members, interacting easily with the chiefs and the wardroom. It all looks so strange to me, to see another commander moving about the ship.

But this is always the way. You command a ship for a period of time—my case a nice long twenty-eight months—and then, in a flash, your time is over. If you care for your ship as I do, you hope for someone like Kevin to come along—smart, and sensible, and clearly a good captain. The *Barry* will be fine without me, I decide, with a slight wrenching feeling in my heart.

During these last days, I walk and walk the ship, savoring the last moments.

The view out over the wintry Virginian capes is gorgeous. The ship moves a bit, but the change of command day is predicted to be clear and still.

Right up to the last, Commodore Morgan tried to talk me into an in-port change of command. "You deserve it," he said. My own view is that the ship will pull into port a couple of weeks before Christmas, and it is an unfair burden on the crew to put on a big production of a change of command at this time of the year, and just a month before deployment.

Colin Powell, in his brilliant autobiography, commented on changes of command by saying, "I could never understand why a thousand men had to stand in the sun for two hours so a couple of O-5s could tell each other how great they were." I agree.

My own view is that a change of command for a ship is about a captain, a crew, and a ship—and the rest is white noise. I'm happy to do this one at sea, very happy indeed.

154 *The Last Day*

I spent the morning walking through my ship one last time. The mess decks. The central control station, where the great engines power this ship. The combat information center, where the brain of Aegis protects us and launches our weapons. The pilot house, scene of so many evolutions, good, bad, and ugly. The forecastle, where the hard-working boatswain's mates are painting away. The fantail, set up for the change of command, a simple ceremony with just the crew, our commodore, and our rear admiral. The wardroom, where I've had over two thousand meals over the past twenty-seven months. And all the special, quiet spots here and there throughout this steel home, where I stopped and chatted for a moment or two with a Sailor about his or her home, or job, or mood, or sense of the ship. God it hurts to leave.

The flight detail was just set, meaning the commodore and the rear admiral will be touching down in fifteen minutes. We'll then simply walk back to the flight deck and say a few words, and it'll be done.

I'll attach my short speech, as it wraps up the many months as well as anything I could dash off now.

Good-bye to the *Barry*. What a sweet ride it was.

155

My change of command speech:

> Adm. Hank Giffin, *George Washington* battle group commander; Commo. John Morgan, commander, DESRON 24 [my immediate boss]; Capt. Ray Pilcher, captain of the *San Jacinto* [my air warfare commander]; Officers, chief petty officers, and crew of the *Barry* . . . my shipmates and friends:

> First of all, I'd like to thank our senior surface warriors in the battle group for coming today for this very simple, at-sea change of command ceremony.

> Admiral Giffin, sir, I have known you for a long time, both ashore and afloat, and I thank you for your patience, your support, and, above all, for the leadership you provide the Navy's premier battle group. I have been fortunate to work with you in the Pentagon, to study alongside you at the War College, and to work for you during this past year in GWBATGRU. Your sense of humor, high standards, and deep professionalism have set a tone in this battle group that will always carry us to victory, no matter the challenge. Thank you for honoring us today with your presence.

Captain Pilcher, throughout my command tour, I have told my watch standers, if we are in formation, and they become confused as to what is going on, follow the lead of the *San Jacinto*. Sir, you command a magnificent ship, one we are proud to work for in the air war organization, and you honor us with your presence today.

Commodore Morgan, you and I have been friends for a very long time indeed; since you were commissioning exec in the *Vincennes* and I was commissioning operations officer in the *Valley Forge*. There is no one in the Navy I would rather have as my change-of-command speaker, and to have served in your squadron for the past year has been the best learning experience and the greatest pleasure of my tour in the *Barry*. Thank you, sir, for coming today to honor the *Barry* with your presence, and especially for speaking today.

Next, I would like to thank Cdr. Kevin Quinn for his professionalism, enthusiasm, and friendship in the long voyage of pipeline training that will culminate today in his assumption of command in the *Barry*. Kevin, I have known you since we were at Annapolis together, and there is not another officer in the Navy to whom I would more gladly surrender command of this exceptional destroyer. We are lucky to have you, sir, and I congratulate you with all my heart. In Nelson's navy, the expression of congratulations was, "I give you joy." And today, my friend, I indeed "give you joy" of your first command.

Most important, I must thank those who are not with us today as we are, so appropriately, at sea: My father, Col. George Stavridis, USMC retired; my mother, Shirley; my father-in-law, retired Navy captain Bob Hall; and my mother-in-law, Joan; as well my children, Christina and Julia; my sister Ann and her daughter Ali. All have helped me with their love and support over the long sea miles of this twenty-seven-month command tour.

Above all, I owe the deepest of debts to my wife Laura, who has been the heart and soul of my command tour as partner, confidante, and, I must admit, my travel companion over much of the Mediterranean last cruise. Although she is not with us today, I willingly acknowledge that nothing I am lucky enough to achieve in my life or my career would be possible without her. Laura, I know you are with me today in your heart, and I thank you for everything.

Shipmates, today is my final day in command of the *Barry*, and I wish with all my heart it were not so. I have been lucky and proud to serve as your captain for twenty-seven months and over 130,000 nautical miles. We have sailed together from the Windward Passage off Haiti to the beaches of Normandy; from the Adriatic Sea during UN air strikes to the harbor of Kuwait City, deep in the Persian Gulf, during Saddam's last aggression toward Kuwait. The *Barry* has been involved in every conceivable operation at sea, from maritime interception to noncombatant extraction; from tracking unknown submarines to rescuing vessels in distress.

A young seaman who walked aboard without a medal in October 1993, would today be wearing the Battle Efficiency ribbon, the Sea Service medal for our deployment, the Southwest Asia Defense Medal for Operation Vigilant Warrior, and the NATO Medal for Operations off Bosnia. We also have been lucky, through the confidence of our seniors and a great deal of good fortune, to win many awards—the Battenberg Cup as the "best all around ship in the Atlantic Fleet"; the Battle Efficiency "E" as the top ship in our destroyer squadron; the Captain Francis F. Ney Award as the top feeder in the Navy; the Rear Admiral Thompson Trophy for Excellence in Communication; and the Golden Anchor for retention, morale, and command atmosphere.

When I reflect back on all we have accomplished in the *Barry*, the reason for our success is very clear: it is standing on the deck of the *Barry* before me. It is a crew, a chiefs' mess, and a wardroom that are a *team*. On the *Barry*, we have always believed that people will almost always turn out to be what you expect. If you treat them as though you expect them to excel, to be men and women of integrity and honor, to work with all their heart for their ship; then they will. It is that simple. The commodore said something to me a few weeks ago that struck me sharply—he said, a "leader is a dealer in hope." A leader is a *dealer in hope*. In the *Barry*, we have tried to foster an atmosphere of quiet competence and professionalism, of friendly enthusiasm, and, above all, an atmosphere of *hope* and belief in the fundamental goodness—indeed, the fundamental excellence—of everyone on board. *Here* we have tried to be *dealers in hope*, at every level, and I think it has made us a solid ship, one to be counted on.

In fact, the highest honor of all my months in command, the one that exceeds by a very great distance any cup or trophy or emblem painted on the side of the ship, was the words spoken to me in the flag cabin on the *George Washington* just over a year ago, by the commander of the *George Washington* battle group. He asked me fly to the carrier, and there he told me that he wanted the *Barry* to escort the carrier into the Persian Gulf in October of 1994, when Saddam Hussein was pushing forces to the border, and we were surging into the Gulf. The *Barry* and the *George Washington* came up to highest speed, and we stayed at that speed, taking fuel from the carrier every thirty-six hours, for six days and forty-two-thousand nautical miles, until we had left the Mediterranean, the Suez, the Red Sea, and the Indian Ocean behind us, and we were come at last to the Persian Gulf. To go to the very end of the spear, when the crisis was real, with the confidence of the battle group commander—that was the highest honor of my tour and indeed of my career thus far. And I think it personifies all that we have tried together to accomplish in the *Barry*—to be a ship that people will choose when the crisis is real and the guns may fire in anger.

What will I miss about being captain in the *Barry*? An easy answer: I will miss my shipmates. In these past twenty-seven months, I have made many, many friends in this ship. Some have moved on; many stand before me today, and I shall miss them all, and that is the real sadness in leaving command. The *Barry* is truly a ship built on friendship, and leaving her is a little like leaving home.

I will miss Mike Franken's humor and efficiency, as well as Charlie Martoglio and Ben Goslin, my previous two execs; and Terry Mosher and Fred Pffirrmann's innovation and competence in running our combat system. I'll miss Vince McBeth's and Bob Kapcio's intelligence and drive as Ops bosses, and Tim Morgan's and Ellen Roberts' dedication and style in supply. I will be sorry to leave behind Russ Wyckoff's wisdom and Dave Dymarcik's wit, and Jerry Roxbury's deep experience—limited duty officers all. I'll be sorry not to see young Lt. Robb Chadwick standing behind the navigation plot, filling me with confidence in my ship, and I will miss Fred Scheib's solid engineering experience, unmatched in my experience.

My chiefs' mess . . . the best. The *Barry* has been blessed with great CPO leadership, from Master Chief Stan Brown, now departed to other duties, to Master Chief Bruce Kennedy, his superb team of senior chiefs, and right through the newest members of the mess. They are a special part of my tour and are truly the heart and soul of the *Barry*.

Above all, I will miss the crew members of the *Barry*. Their smiles and good wishes, their cheerful friendly attitude, and their quiet confidence in their ship and their captain, who certainly had perhaps more than his share of personal doubts along the way, have been the greatest source of strength to me in command.

To paraphrase the Old Testament, those who sail with the crew of the *Barry* do, indeed, "renew their strength; they shall mount up with wings as eagles; they shall run, and not be weary; and they shall walk and not be faint." Shipmates, every day I have spent in the *Barry*, you have renewed my strength and helped me to mount up with wings as eagles; you have let me run and not be weary, and you have shown me how to walk and not be faint . . . no matter the depth of the challenge looming ahead, or the lateness of the hour, or the harshness of the seas we have sailed together.

For all of that, for all you have given this fine ship, I thank you.

Shipmates, a final thought. I think of the *Barry* as a ship with an Irish heart, named for a great Irish-American captain, John Barry, who fought well and true in America's early wars. It has been said that the two defining aspects of the Irish character are good fortune and a great heart. Those are two qualities that this ship shares—good fortune and a great heart. And also like Ireland, the *Barry* has a kind of terrible beauty, with such clean and beautiful lines; and yet so much lethal firepower within this gray steel hull. As my friend Russ Wyckoff has often told me, there truly is a rainbow over this ship, as there is over Ireland so much of the time.

And so I would like to close with the words of a great Irish priest, poet, and scholar, Saint Aidan, who roamed all over Britain and Ireland in the sixth century. He left us a simple poem that is part of the traditional song of the open road of Ireland, and I leave you with his words that capture for me the sadness I feel in leaving all of you and this remarkable ship called the *Barry*:

We always knew it would be so,
That you should stay and I should go.
The sun will set and rise anew,
I wish you well in all you do.

Shipmates and friends, I wish you well in all you do.

Thank you, God bless you, and God bless the good ship *Barry*.

I shall now read my orders.

> From: Chief of Naval Personnel, Washington DC
> To: Commanding Officer, USS BARRY (DDG 52)
> BUPERS Order 3125
> When directed by reporting senior, detach in
> December 1995 and report no later than December
> 1995 to the Joint Staff of the Chairman of the
> Joint Chiefs of Staff, to duty in the Directorate for
> Plans and Policy
> (J-5).

Commander Quinn, I am ready to be relieved. . . .

EPILOGUE

———

I left command of the *Barry* on a sunny winter's day at sea off the coast of Virginia in December of 1996, after more than twenty-seven months in command and over 130,000 sea miles sailed. It was a hard but glorious tour, full of both highs and lows, and above all built on the friendships of a wide variety of wonderful people. Here are how a few of their stories have moved on during the decade and a half since then, as of mid-2007:

Family

Laura, my wife, is, of course, with me in Miami. We've sailed many more thousands of miles together since our days with the *Barry* and have been married for over twenty-five years. She remains the center of my life.

Christina, the eight-year-old daughter of this story, graduates this spring from the University of Virginia, and *Julia* is a fifteen-year-old high school sophomore in Miami. Neither can believe their father is a four-star officer.

My father, retired Marine colonel George Stavridis, passed away in 2001, a few days after 9/11. He remains a figure of importance in the lives of all he touched and is constantly in my thoughts as I work through the challenges of my career and life. My mother, *Shirley*, lives in our family home in Atlantic Beach, Florida, and is in fine health. She continues to be a good friend and neighbor of my wife's parents, *retired Captain and Mrs. Bob Hall*, who likewise enjoy a nice life in Atlantic Beach.

Leaders and Mentors

Vice Adm. Al Krekich, the *George Washington* Battle Group commander, went on to his third star and command of all surface forces in the U.S. Navy. Admiral Krekich, a lineman on the Navy football team with Roger Staubach in the 1960s, continues to be among the most balanced and sensible men I know. He lives and works in the maritime industry in the Norfolk area today.

Vice Adm. Hank Giffin, the second commander of our battle group, was promoted to a third star and given command of all surface forces in the U.S. Atlantic Fleet before retiring to write and consult in the Norfolk area. His successful command tour in the *Thomas S. Gates* remains the standard for command at sea.

Vice Adm. John Morgan, one of four commodores for whom I served, and certainly among the most inspirational leaders for whom I have ever worked, is today a three-star vice admiral and the Navy's operations office on the staff of the chief of naval operations in the Pentagon.

Vice Adm. Kevin Green, good friend and mentor to me throughout this tour and well beyond, retired as a three-star admiral after multiple commands and a stint as the Navy's operations officer in the Pentagon.

Capt. Al Fraser, who remains among my closest and oldest of friends, retired to pursue great business success after commanding the cruiser *Cape St. George* and has become president of Turner Properties in Atlanta, the real estate arm of Ted Turner's far-flung business enterprises.

Friends

Roy Balaconis went on to command the *Mitscher* around the same time I had the *Barry*. He was a swashbuckling figure on the Norfolk waterfront and left the Navy after twenty years as a commander, intent on putting his Tomahawk missile expertise to use in the contractor world. He is very successfully doing that.

Bob Natter continues to be a close friend and adviser who retired as a four-star admiral and commander of Fleet Forces Command.

Mike Lefever was captain in a *Spruance*-class destroyer and had a very successful tour despite the age of the ship he commanded. He is today a one-star rear admiral and recently returned from leading the joint task force in Pakistan that provided humanitarian relief to over a hundred thousand Pakistanis after devastating earthquakes struck that country in 2005. Today he's in Washington, D.C., doing important work on the Navy's personnel management system, and remains a close friend and confidant.

Denis Army commanded the *Arthur W. Radford* and was a fine captain. He went on to command an Aegis-class cruiser as a deep-selected O-6 and was clearly on track to be an admiral in the Navy when tragedy struck. In the prime of his life, this phenomenal athlete contracted ALS (Lou Gehrig's Disease), was crippled, and then suddenly died in his sleep. I went to his funeral in Norfolk, which was in a Catholic church full of the many Sailors and sea captains like me he touched in his life. And it was also full of hundreds of children. Denis, among his many other endeavors, was a frequent youth soccer coach, and the evidence of his gift in that regard was the full pews of teary-eyed youngsters. As I sat in the back of the church that day, I cried too, for all that his family had lost and for all that Denis was denied. He was a fine man and a good friend and shipmate—and the best softball player I ever personally set foot on a diamond with.

Barry Sailors

Adm. Gary Roughead, the commissioning captain of the *Barry*, remains a good friend today. An extraordinarily complete officer, he preceded me to four-star rank and, as of this writing, he has recently taken a new assignment as the chief of naval operations and is off to a brilliant start leading our Navy.

Rear Adm. Kevin Quinn, who relieved me in command of the *Barry*, has gone on to a very successful career, including selection to a second star and assignment to command of a Navy carrier strike group.

Rear Adm. Charlie Martoglio, the commissioning second in command, or executive officer, went on to successfully command his own *Arleigh Burke*–class destroyer, the *Fitzgerald*; has risen to flag rank; and today wears the single star of a rear admiral. He is headed to sea to command a carrier strike group and undoubtedly will move up.

Master Chief Stan Brown retired and is a successful consultant in the Washington, D.C., area.

Capt. Terry Mosher and *Capt. Fred Pffirrmann*, my two superb department heads, both went on to command *Arleigh Burke*–class destroyers with great success, as did *Cdr. Vince McBeth*, our brilliant operations officer. All are moving forward with outstanding success in their careers, and I look for wonderful things from each of them.

Capt. Bob Kapcio, the commissioning operations officer, went on to successful frigate command and is today a commodore at sea operating out of Mayport, Florida.

Capt. Mike Franken, my third executive officer, commanded the *Arleigh Burke*–class destroyer *Winston S. Churchill* and is today a commodore in command at sea.

Cdr. Ben Goslin, my second executive officer, is still on active duty in the Navy, working in Ingleside, Texas.

Cdr. Robb Chadwick, my navigator through thousands of sea miles, has been selected for command at sea and is assigned today to my staff in Miami, Florida, working on strategic communications.

ABOUT the AUTHOR

———

Adm. James Stavridis, commander, United States Southern Command, is a 1976 distinguished graduate of the U.S. Naval Academy and a native of south Florida. A surface warfare officer, he has served at sea in carriers, cruisers, and destroyers.

Admiral Stavridis commanded the destroyer the USS *Barry* (DDG-52) from 1993 to 1995, completing deployments to Haiti, Bosnia, and the Arabian Gulf. The *Barry* won the Battenberg Cup as the top ship in the Atlantic Fleet under his command.

In 1998, he commanded Destroyer Squadron 21 and deployed to the Arabian Gulf, winning the Navy League's John Paul Jones Award for Inspirational Leadership.

From 2002 to 2004, Admiral Stavridis commanded the *Enterprise* Carrier Strike Group, conducting combat operations in the Arabian Gulf in support of both Operation Iraqi Freedom and Operation Enduring Freedom.

Ashore, he served as a strategic and long-range planner on the staffs of the chief of naval operations and the chairman of the Joint Chiefs of Staff. At the start of the Global War on Terror, he was selected as the director of the Navy Operations Group, Deep Blue. He has also served as the executive assistant to the secretary of the Navy and the senior military assistant to the secretary of defense.

Admiral Stavridis earned a PhD and MALD in international relations from the Fletcher School of Law and Diplomacy at Tufts University in 1984, where he won the Gullion Prize as outstanding student. He is also a 1992 distinguished graduate of the National War College.

He holds various decorations and awards, including the Defense Distinguished Service Medal, the Defense Superior Service Medal, and five awards of the Legion of Merit. He is the author or coauthor of several books on shiphandling and leadership, including *Command at Sea*, as well as over a hundred articles published in various professional journals.